MILLION DOLLAR MINDSET

How to Use the Riches of Your Mind to Become Successful

Christine Babbino

MILLION DOLLAR MINDSET: How to Use the Riches of Your Mind to Become Successful

Copyright © 2020 Christine Babbino

ISBN: 979-8-64021-650-9

All rights reserved. No portion of this book may be reproduced mechanically, electronically, or by any other means, including photocopying, without permission of the publisher or author except in the case of brief quotations embodied in critical articles and reviews. It is illegal to copy this book, post it to a website, or distribute it by any other means without permission from the publisher or author.

Limits of Liability and Disclaimer of Warranty
The author and publisher shall not be liable for your misuse of the enclosed material. This book is strictly for informational and educational purposes only.

Warning – Disclaimer
The purpose of this book is to educate and entertain. The author and/or publisher do not guarantee that anyone following these techniques, suggestions, tips, ideas, or strategies will become successful. The author and/or publisher shall have neither liability nor responsibility to anyone with respect to any loss or damage caused, or alleged to be caused, directly or indirectly by the information contained in this book.

Publisher
10-10-10 Publishing
Markham, ON Canada

Printed in Canada and the United States of America

Contents

Dedication	v
Foreword	vii
Acknowledgements	ix
Chapter 1: Million Dollar Mindset 101	1
Chapter 2: Standing in the Face of Fear	9
Chapter 3: Overcoming Anger and Sadness	17
Chapter 4: Failure and Establishing a Winning Attitude	35
Chapter 5: Passion Is Priceless and So Are You	49
Chapter 6: Why You Should Be Successful	61
Chapter 7: Amplify Kindness	73
Chapter 8: Energy, Momentum, and Discipline	85
Chapter 9: Glorifying Gratitude	101
Chapter 10: Welcome to the Winners Circle	111

I dedicate this book to every person out there who is looking for success and doesn't know where to find it. I also dedicate this book to anyone who is enthusiastic about changing their lifestyle and the way they think in terms of their prosperity.

Foreword

Are you happy with where you are in life right now? Or are you stagnant and so caught up in life's distractions that you have no idea what you want to do, or where you want to go? Do you want to succeed in everything that you put your mind to? Do you want to learn how to use the riches of your mind to become extremely successful? If so, you have come to the right place.

No matter who you are, or what your current status is mentally or financially, *Million Dollar Mindset* will help shape up your mind for tremendous success. This book is full of information and steps to get you moving forward on the road to success. When it comes to doing what you love, what is holding you back? You. That is the only thing keeping you from achieving your dreams.

In the end, your mindset is the only thing that is standing between you and your final dream destination. *Million Dollar Mindset* will set you on a course to be a more, positive and happy individual inside and out. It will show you ways to combat specific barriers that have been holding you back for years, and teach you how to manipulate them to your advantage. *Million Dollar Mindset* shows you how to use your mind as a weapon to succeed in everything that you have ever wanted.

Author Christine Babbino has gone from a persistent negative thinker to someone who has created a more positive and successful lifestyle, based on the strategies she puts into practice daily. Christine puts into perspective all of her blueprints on how to overcome fear, using her own past experiences and encounters. Throughout this book, Christine also shows you different dynamics on how to approach underlying emotions such as anger and sorrow, in order to set yourself up for massive success in the long run.

If you want to win big, this book is for you. I highly recommend *Million Dollar Mindset* if you want to drastically change your life for the better. After reading this book, you will feel empowered to take on the world with a whole new passion, especially with the advanced tactics you will learn and put to use.

Raymond Aaron
New York Times Bestselling Author

Acknowledgements

I would first like to thank my parents, **Nanette Babbino** and **Frank Babbino,** for helping me become who I am today. Thank you for showing me so much support, especially with writing my book, and all the other success programs that I am invested in. I am eternally grateful for the encouragement and positive attitude that led me to be who I am today. I couldn't have been this successful without such amazing parents. Thank you for raising me to be a leader and to follow my dreams to my greatest ability. For this, I am forever thankful.

I would also like to thank all four of my older sisters, **Trisha Babbino, Barbara Mitchell, Tammy Babbino,** and **Andrea Babbino,** for setting such great examples for me growing up. If I aspired to be anyone, it would be any four of you guys. As I was the youngest, you guys paved the way for me to see what it was like to be independent. Watching all of you grow older and taking on roles of responsibility, it showed me what it was like to be responsible and take on things for myself. I will forever be grateful for your advice and guidance.

Thank you to all of my nephews—**Christopher, Anthony, Derrick, Alex,** and **Daniel**—and also to my sole niece, **Destiny.** You guys have taught me what it's like to set an example. As an aunt, I always felt like I had to be a role model for all of you while growing up. I am so proud of the young men and woman that you have become today, and I hope that I serve, and continue to serve, as a great role model for all of you in the future. Thank you, **Anthony**, for your unwavering devotion and dedicated service to our country. We all greatly appreciate it and will never forget the hard work that you have accomplished.

Thank you to my brother-in-law, **David Mitchell**, for always giving me good advice on where to go in life. You always seemed to help me when I was confused the most. By the end of the day, I always felt like I had it all sorted out, which brought me a sense of comfort and relief when I needed it the most. Thank you for being a light in the darkness and a guidance figure that I can count on. I am eternally grateful for your guidance in my life.

Of course, I would also like to acknowledge all of my friends that I used to work with—**Madeline**, **Andrea**, **Trish**, **Destiny**, **Diane S.**, **Diane F.**, **Kim**, **Narcisa**, **Adosinda**, **Alice**, **Tina**, **Kimberley S.**, **Jim**, **Luis**, **Brian**, **David V.**, **Dave O.**, **Rich**, **John**, **Jeff**, and **Eric L.**—and store owners, **Eric S.** and **Jessica S.** I would like to thank all of you for your consistent support and advice when I needed it the most. I will never forget all of the memories we've had together, and all of the laughs that we shared every day to just get through the day. Thank you for your words of encouragement and all of the faith that you had in me to excel and do better. I couldn't have worked with a better group of people.

I would also like to thank the late **Joseph F. Lisicky Jr.**, for being my best friend through thick and thin. Although you will never get the chance to see this, I know you are smiling down from heaven as my guardian angel, and watching me grow. You have inspired me to be a better person and step outside of my comfort zone to achieve bigger and better things. You have always been

Acknowledgements

the person that I looked back on whenever I felt like giving up. You have always been my main source of motivation, and the reason why I continue to improve who I am every day. I will never forget all of the times that we shared together, and I will always be your number one fan. Thank you for all of the wonderful memories.

I would also like to thank all my past teachers and professors from high school and college. Thank you for teaching me to be a better person and to make the right life choices. Your guidance has helped me grow in more ways than one, and for that I am truly grateful. Thank you for all the knowledge you have passed on to me, and all the wisdom that you have provided me with on my journey. I will never forget the sacrifices you have all made for the sake of your students. It's time to pass on the knowledge that you all have taught me as well. You are all the reason why I am paying it forward.

Thank you to my dear friend, **Rosemary**, for supporting me throughout the years on all my endeavors. You continue to inspire me to become a better version of myself every day, and I couldn't be more grateful. You consistently push me to be a better person and to always shoot for the stars, no matter what I do. You will always be a dear friend of mine, and I am thankful to have you in my life.

I would like to thank my dear friend, **David Strelecki**, for seeing the good in me as a person. You showed me the greatness in "paying it forward," and in continuing to give to those that you don't even know, without explanation. Thank you for being a good friend of mine, and for always making me laugh when I need a good joke. You will always be a great part of my life and, because of you, I will always continue to pay it forward.

Thank you, **Raymond Aaron,** for providing me with the great program to become a published author. I couldn't have been more grateful to receive an opportunity such as this. It is an amazing experience to have someone such as you write my foreword and be my coach. When I arrived at the seminar that you were speaking at in Dallas, I never thought I would be walking out as an almost published author. I am eternally grateful for the services you have provided me with, as well as for the chance to get myself branded as an authority figure. Thank you for everything that you have done.

I would also like to thank **Tony Robbins**, for being my role model as the world's top life coach. As a life coach on the rise, you have been my main inspiration for my career choice. I have always looked up to you as this smart, genuine, and caring guy, who cares about the well-being of others. I continuously strive to be like you every day, in hopes that I can impact the world in the same way you did. Thank you for being my mentor and role model.

Thank you, **Gary Vaynerchuk,** for turning my life around in a tremendous way. You've opened my eyes to a lot of things that I didn't notice until I started watching your content. You showed me the importance of spreading love and kindness. You have also showed me how to be thankful for the things that I have currently, and to not look for more than I need. You have inspired me to find my passion in life and to chase it, no matter how many odds are set against me. You have also showed me that happiness is true success, unlike what others may believe. Thank you for being a huge role model for me, and for helping me change my life for

Acknowledgements

the better.

I would also like to thank **Donald Trump**, for showing me the importance of thinking big and having a winning attitude. You have showed me that in order to be successful, it all has to start with your mindset. You have also inspired me to reach my full potential, and to know that leaving behind a legacy is the greatest thing that you can ever do in this world. Your books have taken me to another level of thinking, and this has disciplined me to have the powerful mindset that I continue to have today. Thank you for being such a great role model.

Chapter 1
Million Dollar Mindset 101

"Your mind is your weapon, your power.
Your thoughts are powerful enough to move the world...
you just have to believe they are."
~ Unknown

    In order to achieve a goal or become a success, we must take into consideration the thing that gets us there: our mindset. The mind is a very powerful attribute that can determine if we are going in the right direction, or in a direction that we never wanted to be in the first place. We were all born with a very gracious gift, the gift of our minds. Our minds are very powerful weapons that can either set us up for success or failure, based on how we utilize it. It doesn't matter if you are financially rich or poor. You have all of the riches you will ever need, when you have your family, your health, and the power of your mind to manifest and make things happen. But the challenge is up to you to make things happen. It's your choice entirely, whether you use it for success or for something else other than success.

    Positive thinking plays a very crucial role in getting from point A to B in our lives. If you look at almost every successful person on the face of this planet, I guarantee that each and every one of them will tell you that having and keeping a positive, disciplined mindset is the key to becoming a success. Have you ever wondered why people who are consistently negative stay stuck where they are? That's the answer! They constantly feed their minds with negativity, and negative results are what they get back in return. Throughout my journey in becoming a life coach, I have noticed that if I kept positive even in the most negative situations, I won. The more positive thoughts I fed my mind, the more positive results flowed my way. I even came up with a quote for myself that has helped me through times of struggle: "Feed your mind well, and it will feed you tenfold." It's true. The more positivity you feed your mind, the more positive results you will see, the more of a success you will be, and ultimately, the happier you will be. But habits and discipline also play a crucial role in becoming successful. You can be the most positive human being on Earth and still not achieve your goals. Why? Because action and execution are also important factors in becoming a success, but none of those are possible without the proper mindset and motivation to get you started.

Our minds are very powerful tools that determine our failures and successes, how we face those outcomes, and how we build upon ourselves and become a better person because of those results. What you feed your mind on a daily basis is what you will get in return. If you think about garbage, you will produce garbage. If you think about becoming a success and actually put the work in habitually every day to do so, you will become a success. Just as we have to supply our bodies with the daily nutrition of food, glucose, and carbohydrates to keep functioning, we have to do the same thing with our minds. If you feed your body junk food, candy, and soda every day, you will eventually end up overweight and at risk for a stroke or heart attack. Feed your body with healthy meals, fruits, vegetables, and water, followed by exercise, and I guarantee you will not only look better, but you will feel better as a result. The same thing happens with our minds! If you consistently feed your mind every day with nasty thoughts about yourself, such as, "I can't do this," or "I can never do that," then guess what will happen? You will never accomplish whatever it is you want to do! Why? Because you fed your mind junk food instead of feeding it the correct nutrition it needs to function properly. Ratan Tata once quoted something that I have found to be very true throughout my journey: *"No one can destroy iron, but its own rust can. Likewise, no one can destroy a person, but their own mindset can."* I agree with this quote 100%. No one can destroy himself mentally, but man can. This is why mindset and positive thinking are so important to one's success.

At one point in my life, I was a habitual negative thinker. At certain times in my life, I still am, but I have learned to correct myself every time a thought like that comes my way. How can you correct yourself? By taking the statements such as "I can't do this," or "I can never do that," and rearranging the words a little bit. Instead, try saying, "I can do this," or "I can always do that." A switch in a couple of words in your thoughts every day, can lead to major results in the long run. I remember that my former computer teacher in high school used to talk about this term called "GIGO." Although he was referring to the programming of a PC computer, it stood for "Garbage in, garbage out." This never struck me as a computer term but rather as a way to express what goes into your mind and what comes out as a result of what you put in. Of course, he was talking about programming a computer, but I took it as a life lesson instead of a computer lesson.

Your environment also plays a crucial role in the empowerment of your mindset and your daily thoughts. Who you hang around with is who you will eventually become. If you hang out with five millionaires, you will eventually become the sixth. If you hang out with drug dealers, you eventually become one too, not to mention serving time in prison if you get caught. My father always taught me one thing as a kid: "If you hang with the lame, you will become lame." I have never found this to be truer in my life. Throughout my years in college, I met so many people who consistently fed their minds with so much gossip, drama, and complaining, that it was all that they focused on. These are the kind of people that did not end up getting very far with their goals. They were so focused on everyone else's lives that they forgot to focus on who they were as a person and on reaching their own goals. They fed their minds with so much negativity that they forgot to believe in themselves and all of the great things that they were capable of achieving. These people also hung around in crowds that thought the same way, and it affected them too. I've known so many great, joyous, and positive individuals that were on the right track towards their success and goals, who automatically destroyed their lives because of just one negative person they hung around.

I knew this one kid in high school that took a turn for the worse because of who they decided to hang around. This individual was a bright, straight-A student, with remarkable credentials to show for it, and they were loved by almost every teacher in the school. By the time college rolled around, this kid had decided to hang around with someone not so great, and someone who was heavily into drugs. This remarkable kid, who was capable of doing great things, was now in prison on major drug charges. I have also seen the opposite scenario play out in cases where people, who had hung out in not such great crowds, turned their lives around completely by hanging out with one positive and successful person. This applied to me as well. In high school, I was never the straight-A student, until I started hanging around with a totally different crowd. In the beginning, I was your average B and C student. I hung around with the students who really didn't care much for their grades or putting in any effort. But one day, when I was staring at my report card and hearing everyone else talking about all the great colleges they were going to get into, I knew it was time for a change. Reality hit me hard on thoughts of what I may be doing with the rest of my life after high school. I took into account what my father had taught me, and let that sink in.

That very day, I decided it was time to apply myself to my studies habitually, and what better way to learn how to do so than hanging out with the honors and straight-A crowd. So that was exactly what I did. Once I started hanging with the straight-A crowd, I started to learn how to think like them, how to study like them, what they were into, and more importantly, how to achieve the same results that they were achieving as well—I observed. Within a year or so, I jumped from being 64th in my class, to 32nd in my class, in such a short period of time. By senior year, I was in the top 20% of my class, with all first and distinguished honors awards every quarter. When I reached college, I did the exact same thing and applied the exact same strategy. I walked across that stage to achieve my associate's degree with high honors and a 3.8 GPA, and being able to get into almost every college that I had applied to. I was even able to tutor other students in classes that I had taken and excelled in. It felt great! It was all due to who I hung around with and what I kept my focus on. As the old saying goes, "You are what you eat," and this applies to the mind as well. Hang around positive and successful people, who consistently feed your mind with positive thoughts, as well as doing it for yourself, and you will become unstoppable. Positive results will automatically flow in your direction.

I give all this credit to my mindset. It was what I fed my mind day in and day out, who I chose to hang around with in my environment, and what my motivating factor was. Passion also plays a big role when you are looking to crush your goals. What are you doing this for? Where do you see yourself in the future, and who are you aiming to become? If you don't have passion for what you do, you might as well throw all your hard work and dedication right out the window. Having passion for what you do is everything. It determines what is going to make you happy in the long term. Let me ask you this: If you are not happy with what you are doing, then why are you doing it? If you are doing it for the money, stop. Yes, you may be rich in the end, but will you be happy? I don't think so. I know that I'd rather be happy with what I am doing than be rich. In fact, I'd rather get rich doing what I love. According to the ancient philosopher, Aristotle, *"Achieving happiness is the highest human good."* It's what almost every individual aspires to be in the end: happy. If you are not happy with what you do, you need to change it immediately. Because if you are not happy with what you do, you will never cook up the positive thoughts required for you to get there, and in the long run, you may never end up getting there. This is why having passion for what you do is important. Loving what I do every day, and leaving a legacy behind with it, would never make me happier.

Throughout the course of this book, I will go on to talk about some barriers that prevent people from producing a positive mindset, and how to overcome them through simple, easy steps. Most people never reach their goals because of these barriers. You can have a positive mindset all you want, but there will always be an obstacle to face that will try to tear that down. Whether it be fear, anger, sadness, or failure, as human individuals, we all face some sort of emotion throughout our daily lives. But being disciplined to keep a positive mindset in the face of a bunch of negative situations, is something only a warrior can do. I will also show you how to establish and keep a positive mindset so that you will be able to soar and excel in anything that you do. Greatness exists within all of us, and with the right attitude and mindset, you can become completely unstoppable.

Chapter 2

Standing in the Face of Fear

*"Fear is just an obstacle. Fear is what makes us humans great.
Fear is nothing than just an imagination!
Face what you fear and make what you fear, fear you."*
~ Mark R. Bergren

Most people find excuses for why they can't and don't want to succeed. It is because something either externally or internally is blocking them from continuing to do what they love. What is stopping them exactly? It's called fear. What is fear? The actual textbook definition of fear is the anticipation of pain. A lot of people are scared of going through with their success, because they fear what may happen next, or what other people may think about them. There are many other factors for why someone might fear becoming successful. Fear could be internal, where someone may think that if they get rich, they may lose all of their money; or they may even doubt their capability to accomplish something. External fear is when an outside force or obstacle is keeping you from achieving what you truly desire. For example, fear of what your friends may think of you if you became successful or rich, or fear that you may outgrow everyone else in your career path, and suddenly you may think that most of your friendships will be terminated because of it. Fear is just that, the anticipation of pain. A lot of individuals do not want to move on with their success because they are anticipating that some kind of pain lies on the other side as a consequence of becoming successful.

Fear plays an essential role in survival, and dates back to the most ancient of generations. Whether it be slaying a mammoth for dinner, or killing a lion that is attacking you, fear was by far the largest emotion that individuals were faced with back in the days of the Stone Age. Currently, fear still exists, just not as prevalent as the ways of the Stone Age, because of advancements in technology, and different ways of hunting. Fear, today, is expressed more as social fear. Whether it be fearing the loss of a job or a relationship, the emotion of fear has evolved significantly over the centuries. The fight-or-flight response activated by our peripheral nervous system, is a way of responding to fear as an adrenaline rush. This kind of fear is more "in the moment," such as being startled by someone that you didn't know was behind you, or getting into a fist fight with someone in the spur of the moment. This type of a response is normal, and it is part of the stress response system that we are initially born with.

Fear is a mindset. Just as any other emotion we feel, it is something that every human being experiences. We could choose to continue to let it override our desires, or we can override it ourselves by telling ourselves that it is just an emotion that every human being feels at some point, and we will not let it stand in the way of our dreams! Out of all the emotions that we let stand in the way of our positive thinking and goals, fear is the biggest one. Fear is the reason why ninety-five percent of people quit before they even start. When we are born, we are initially born with two types of fear: the fear of falling and the fear of loud noises—everything else is learned. That fear of spiders you may have when walking down the basement steps? It is learned at an early age. That fear of the walls closing in on you in such a small, cramped space? It is learned as well. When we are young, we are exposed to many different factors as to why we fear certain things. For instance, as a child, if you ever went to a classmate's birthday party, only to turn around and be startled for an instant by a tall, scary man with a painted-up face and rainbow hair, you may have developed a life-long fear of clowns. I know so many people who have always had a life-long fear, which could be reverted back to a minor situation that occurred when they were younger.

On the upside, there are also very many people who enjoy fear. Enjoy fear? You may wonder how this is even a possibility. In fact, many people purposely induce fear daily. Whether it be jumping from a plane or watching scary movies, some individuals actually do this to enjoy the adrenaline rush. Many race car drivers experience fear all of the time. Racing at high speeds and cutting corners, knowing that there is a chance that they might crash into a wall or into another car, takes guts. Most race car drivers do this to induce their fear, because they adamantly enjoy the adrenaline rush that the sport entails. Crazy, right? But this is also a tactic that people use to eradicate their fears. Some people face their fear by looking at it directly in the eye and taking it head-on. In psychology, this is actually known as exposure therapy. In the past, patients that had a severe fear of spiders, who were slowly exposed to the arachnids at different therapy sessions, were eventually cured of their fear by being exposed to the actual thing they were afraid of. I myself actually encourage this technique; I use it whenever a new fear arises. It is a way of telling my mind that I will not tolerate this fear to become a part of me and hold me back.

Fear can lead a lot of people in the wrong direction and on the wrong paths in their careers. They play the "safe" game. Some people would rather pick a safe career that will make them a living, than go for what they really love to do, regardless if it makes them a fortune or if it makes them live below their means for a short period of time. As a biology and pre-medical major in college, I was looking at the dollar signs of what the career had to offer financially in the long run. I liked the subject and found it interesting, but I wasn't actually looking at what I loved to do, which was life coaching and motivational speaking. The medical field is also a highly competitive major; every student in the class wants to be the smartest and most academically astute student in the class. I also fell into that trap. Seeing everyone else earning their straight A's and keeping their 4.0 GPA's, I grew jealous because I wanted to do better than them. I was so afraid of failing at times, I would beat myself up for even one or two questions incorrectly answered on an exam. I was motivated by fear and jealousy. I wasn't motivated by passion; I was motivated by dollar signs, a fear of failing, and just by wanting to be better than every other student in that major. If someone had even a slightly higher GPA than I had, I grew envious of that person.

I found my true passion while going through the trials and tribulations of experiencing what it was like to be a medical student. I had to keep motivated somehow, knowing how hard and intense of a major it was. That is where I fell in love with motivation and self-empowerment. I enjoyed it so much that I wanted to help others as well. This is where my call for becoming a life coach came into play. Coincidence, right? While I thought I was doing what I loved, I was actually being blinded by the money and having a considerable reputation. I found my true calling by being tested. How God works in mysterious ways, I will never know.

This was all because fear led me down the wrong path, and I finally opened my eyes to it when I attended the Millionaire Mind Intensive seminar. This is an example of how fear and playing the "safe" game can lead a lot of people to just want to make a living, and not to be doing exactly what they would love to be doing. I've seen numerous, bright individuals in college give up what they really love to do, because of three things: They were either letting the dollar signs blind them; choosing their career because of what society thought was socially acceptable; or they were scared of what their parents might think of them if they wanted to do what they loved, and not what their parents wanted them to be. All of these scenarios are driven by fear, and once we let fear grab a hold of us, it is difficult to realize that we are encompassed by it, therefore making it a million times harder to let go of the emotion.

When I attended the Millionaire Mind Intensive seminar awhile back, we learned how fear is the number one reason why people don't go through with their dreams. We did an exercise that consisted of a wooden arrow with a metal tip. On the arrow, we had to write down what we had to break through in spite of fear, in order to achieve our goals. I wrote down on my arrow: old habits, procrastination, old ways of thinking, negativity, and so on and so forth. The purpose of this exercise was to break through the things that were holding you back because of fear. During this exercise, we had someone hold the back of the arrow, while you put the tip right in the small pocket of your throat. You had to imagine that all of your goals and ambitions were on the other side of that arrow, and that you had to break through your old ways in spite of fear, if you wanted to achieve your goals. Acting in spite of fear is crucial if you want to achieve everything that you have ever dreamed of. I have seen so many people quit before they were even ahead, because they were scared of what their mom thought of them, or because they thought the success would be too much to handle for them, and they might end up losing it all. If you do not break through your fear, you will stay stuck in your old ways and habits, which will only lead to further negativity, and you will never achieve your dreams.

 I used to doubt myself all of the time, before I knew what it took to become successful. I used words such as, "What if," or "I can't do this because." Utilizing these phrases can be dangerous, allowing you to slide down a slippery slope of negativity and end up stuck in a pit of fear. That's why I think rephrasing words is crucial to maintaining a positive mindset and taking action towards your goals. Catching yourself in the act, and rephrasing your words, rewires your brain to tell it that this type of a mindset is void and no longer acceptable. It will take some time, dedication, and discipline, of course; but it will eventually lead you to a mindset that is more enriching, fulfilling, and more positive overall. Right now, if you are sitting here thinking that it is ultimately impossible to rephrase your thoughts—stop. You are letting excuses override your aspirations, and that is just another point that your brain is wired a certain way in negativity to keep you fearful. Your brain

Standing in the Face of Fear

did that on purpose, and it's time to let go of that fear that has been holding you back for some time now. The more you tell yourself that you "can't," you won't, and you're just letting failure enter into your life willingly. But if you rephrase your words and tell yourself that you "can," you are inviting a winning attitude to be instilled in your brain, making it ten times easier to achieve whatever it is that you want to achieve!

So, how do we diminish the emotion of fear when it comes to being successful? You cannot fully eradicate the emotion, but you can override it by choosing to break through old patterns, habits, and negative ways of thinking that have been holding you back for years on end. First of all, if you care about what people will think about you when you do become successful, you're letting other peoples' opinions dictate your life. You automatically give up control over your own life and happiness when you allow someone else's negative opinions to affect you and govern your actions. This could prevent you from achieving your goals. Stop letting other people dictate your happiness, when you are 100% in full and entire control of your life. You are the captain of your own ship, and you steer yourself towards your own destiny. Now, it's time to grab a hold of that fear and show it who is boss. You are in control of you, not your fear. Remember that fear is only a mindset, and so is positivity. It's time to replace the concept of fear with something positive and more affirmative. You need to tell yourself that you are in control, and not whatever it is that the fear might be. It's time to break through old habits that have been holding you back from your goals, and to create new and exciting strategies that get you to where you want to be. Once you become fearless, life becomes limitless. This can never be more accurate. Once you make your goals and aspirations a million times more important than the fear that is holding you back, you become limitless to all the opportunities out there that await you to seize them. Everything you have ever dreamed about—your goals, your aspirations, your vision, and your success—lies on the other side of that arrow. So, I think it's about time to take a brisk step into that arrow, in spite of fear, negativity, old habits, and pain. It's time to step forth into abundance, joy, gratitude, and happiness. Your dreams are just on the other side of that arrow. What are you waiting for? Go for it.

Chapter 3

Overcoming Anger and Sadness

"Holding on to anger is like grasping a hot coal with the intent of throwing it at someone else; you are the one who gets burned."
~ Buddha

Everyone has experienced some sort of anger in their lives, and some on a daily basis. Anger is just another one of the many types of emotions that can lead us to live unfulfilling and unsuccessful lives, if we let it get the best of us. We have all had rough days, or days that made us want to punch someone in the face, who said something nasty to us that they shouldn't have. But before we delve into what anger really is, and how to assess it, we need to know the real definition of anger. According to psychology, anger is an emotion characterized by antagonism toward someone or something you feel has deliberately done you wrong. Have you ever had a time where you left your lunch in the refrigerator at work and went to retrieve it at break time, only to find out that someone had eaten it? How angry did that make you feel? Pretty angry, right? I know I would feel angry if someone stole my food! Anger can also turn into what is known as excessive anger. Excessive anger can cause a multitude of problems that affect your mental and physical health. This type of anger could increase blood pressure and could cause you to think unclearly when making decisions. That is why most angry bosses, who yell at their employees and make them feel inferior, have a high turnover rate and usually have unsuccessful businesses, because they make all of their decisions when they are angry and can't think clearly.

The emotion of anger usually involves a second individual that has caused you to feel this way. The reason that people get angry is because some other party has either said or done something to ruin the other person's self-esteem, or committed an injustice that causes them to lose their patience. Anger is often accompanied by hostile thoughts and aggressive behaviors if the situation is large enough. It can interfere with relationships, work performance, mental and physical well-being, as well as taking you off track with your goals. You lose your focus entirely. I knew someone who was so angry with life and what he was going through, that he decided that there was only one way to end all of the pain. Of course, suicide is never the answer; and fortunately, it was all talk and no action for him. He is doing fine and is well as of today, but the point is, if you don't get to the source of why you are angry, and fix it right away, it could lead to a whole life spiral, right down the tubes!

In high school, this one kid that was failing a class asked the teacher for extra credit to improve his grade so he could pass the class. The teacher rejected the student's wishes and denied him the extra credit, telling him that he never did the homework for the class. The kid was so furious that he stormed out of the classroom and slammed the door shut behind him, which created a loud banging noise that scared the heck out of all of us. This sent vibrations through the room that caused loose and light objects to almost scream Geronimo as they fell right off the shelves! Boy, was that kid furious! I never knew what happened to that kid and his grade in the class after that, but the point is that anger could lead to negative thoughts that try to grab a hold of who we are, instead of us controlling the emotion ourselves. This could lead to unhealthy patterns in our lives that can cause us to be unsuccessful.

What truly matters is how we deal with our anger and come up with solutions that are more positive and healthy in return, for both parties at hand. What happened when that kid stormed out of the room was that he allowed his teacher to take control of how he felt. When you become angry at someone, you automatically let them take control of your feelings and your happiness, and you basically let them dictate how you feel. If someone is trying to bring you down and says something to you out of spite, with a smile on their face, just know that misery loves company, and those who are trying to bring you down are already beneath you. I've dealt with plenty of people like that, and it had nothing to do with myself; it was just the fact that these people were so angry at themselves, for some other reason in their lives, that they wanted to take their hostility out on someone else. Most of the time, these people do it because they feel insecure about themselves. They may feel insignificant, unloved, or unimportant to you. There are numerous reasons why someone might try and hurt you. Know that they didn't mean to hurt you; know that it came from the insecurities within themselves that they need to take care of it, not you. Always be willing to forgive, because most people don't even notice that they are doing it. But most of all, forgive yourself, because the anger isn't hurting them; it is hurting you first and foremost. Nelson Mandela once quoted, *"Resentment is like drinking poison and then hoping it will kill your enemies."* This couldn't be more accurate. When we get angry over what someone else has done to us, it does not affect them at all. The anger is killing you inside, instead of the person you want it to affect.

The key, whenever you feel like you are getting angry towards someone who caused you harm, and you know you didn't do anything wrong, is to keep your head held high and keep smiling. Know that it has nothing to do with you, and most likely has everything to do with them. Remember, once you let someone else dictate your happiness, it is the moment you lose control of your happiness, and to someone you may not even be in contact with five years from now. Also remember that if it won't matter in five years, why are you even letting it affect you for five minutes?

This is why anger can be so futile. I knew a person that was so angry over their ex, that they let the emotion take over their entire life. This person ended up ruining other friendships they had, switching to an unfulfilling career, and in the end, causing themselves to lose money and a house that they owned. They financially ended up in a hole because of the resentment they had towards someone else. It led them to lose focus and to make destructive life decisions. Just because you are angry at someone else, does not mean you should take it out on others as well. That third party that you may have taken something out on, may get hurt or upset as well, and they could be completely innocent. Words can hurt someone mentally, so when you are angry, you also need to be careful of how you treat others. This is why so many angry people end up losing great friendships that they might have had for years. I am going to show you how to manage your anger better, in ways that won't hurt you or your friendships, and to train your mind how to turn anger into positivity. I will be using examples from my own life and from those of my clients that I've mentored in the past.

Going back a couple of years ago, I was criticized for the way I looked. Being born premature, I had to deal with growth issues all my life; I have a shorter and more petite stature than most other females my age. While everyone else in high school was wearing clothes that made them look like growing women, I was not able to fit in any of them due to my stature. I felt embarrassed and not like the other girls that were my age. Up until this day, I still have a petite stature, but this time I was faced with criticism. I was told that I'd never be able to find someone my age that would like me, due to my size. Needless to say, I was angry. But it's how I dealt with that anger that mattered. I decided to take my anger and use it as leverage towards something positive. Being a college student at the time, I had mountains of homework, and tests to study for, so I decided to take it out on my homework instead of taking it out on someone else. That night, I went home and started working on college algebra assignments, telling myself that if I didn't work out the problem and get the correct answer, I would make myself look at examples of the same type of problem with different numbers, and try them all until I got them right. That is exactly what I did for each and every problem, until I had not missed one question. When it came time for the exam, I scored a 99.9%, only because I missed one zero somewhere along the line, but it was an honest mistake, and I was not mad at all. I was just very happy that I basically aced the exam. But the point of the whole story is that I took my anger and put it into a positive action, which then resulted in a positive outcome. After that, I found that I was not angry anymore about what was said to me. I was just happy about the fact that I had got an A on my exam, which ended up raising my grade for the entire class. Who knew that taking one negative emotion and turning it into a positive action could be so rewarding? It was in that moment that I realized that if I could do that, I could control every other negative emotion the exact same way and turn it into something successful. If I could do that with a measly exam grade, I could do it on much bigger levels financially. Using your anger as leverage, to your advantage, could bring massive results in the long haul. Anger is an emotion that everyone experiences, but learning how to use it to your advantage, is not something that many people know how to do.

Communication is always a key factor in releasing anger as well. Telling the other individual how you feel about the situation, may release those negative feelings all at once. It is a good stress reliever if the other party takes into account your feelings as well, and reciprocates their side of the story. But that is not always the case. You may speak your feelings out to a person, and they may end up angry and starting an argument. Also, remind yourself that this is not your fault, and that you did what you needed to do to get those thoughts off your chest. If they want to feel angry that you tried to resolve something, that is entirely on them. In the end, you will still feel much better for trying to get the situation resolved, and how you feel, off your mind.

I can remember a time that I was furious at someone for ruining a great friendship of mine by spreading lies and rumors about me, instead of telling the truth, to make themselves look like the hero of the story. Inside, I was enraged for months, until I finally confronted the situation. I needed to let the anger out. I ended up messaging the person about how angry I was at them for ruining a friendship that I had for years, just because they wanted to make themselves look like the big shot. The response I got back, from the long, extensive paragraph that I had sent, was only "Ok," but I still felt much better than I did previously. In fact, I felt like the weight of the world had been lifted off my shoulders. I also felt that if they didn't want to resolve the situation, then that would be on them, but I would no longer let the negative emotions affect my decisions. If someone wants to let a situation remain unresolved, let them; but speak your piece. They are only allowing their insecurities to override who they are as a person themselves. Remember that only you yourself can choose to feel better if you want to. If they don't want to be helped, then you can't force them—they have to want to feel better themselves.

The point is that even if you get a short response back, or even no response at all, it still feels a hell of a lot better to get those nasty emotions off your chest, no matter how rude the second party may be in replying to what you have to say. Anger is like putting pounds of gaseous pressure into a plastic bottle and keeping it capped: If you don't release whatever is on your mind, you are bound to explode at some point. It is like keeping poison inside of you and expecting it to just go away—it won't. You need to get the treatment you need, in order to get the toxins out of your system, to feel better and move on with your daily activities. Have you ever felt the effects of food poisoning? It's terrible, isn't it? You go out and have a great dinner, and early the next morning when you wake up, all of a sudden your stomach is doing backflips ten times over, to the point where you don't even want to get out of bed. You end up calling off work, losing money, and getting backed up with work for a day or two, until you treat it properly and feel better again. Anger works in the same respect, except if you don't get to the solution and treat it properly, it can turn into a downward spiral and sicken you mentally. This is the reason why some people who remain angry at something for years, end up ruining everything else in their lives. They let the poison sicken them to the point where it hurts their daily functions and affects them in all other aspects of their lives.

For example, some people that have failed in their businesses may have lost their marriages as well, because they didn't manage one loss the right way, and they let it interfere with their relationships. The effect can work the opposite as well, and I want to prevent it from happening to you. Get to the solution of whatever it is, and handle it right away. If you don't, it could affect other areas in your life that you don't want it to hurt. When I was angry at that person for ruining my friendship, I wasn't motivated to do anything else within my daily functions. I was so caught up on this one situation that it enveloped everything else that I was capable of doing, and I basically told my brain that it was not important. When I finally took notice of what was happening, I had to do something. Even messaging this person in order to get what I needed to say off my mind, made me feel 100% better, and I was back to doing what I loved five minutes later, feeling absolutely relieved.

There was a nasty argument between two coworkers at my job one time, and it was so bad that you could actually see the steam coming out of the ears of both parties. This situation went on for days, and neither of the individuals spoke to each other unless it was work related. You could see the anger in both of these individuals just by the expression on their faces. One of the individuals finally spoke up and asked, "So, when are you going to talk to me again?" This made the other individual blow her cap and express exactly how she felt about the situation. To keep it confidential, I will not go into details about the situation, and I will not get into who was right in the argument, out of dignity and respect, but I chose this example to make a point. When my coworker was finished saying her side of the story and how she felt about what was going on, I could tell immediately that she felt relieved about letting it out. The situation may have not been resolved completely, but I could tell that she felt so much better by just letting the poison out of her system. Sometimes we need to get down to what is bothering us so that we can function properly, and to our fullest potential. There is also another emotion that can hinder us and hold us back if we don't treat it properly, and it goes hand in hand with anger. That emotion is called sadness.

Sadness affects us all at some point or another; it's how we deal with that emotion, and the situations, that matters the most. Variations of sadness can be on a wide range scale, from something small that got you upset, to even being trauma related. An example of something small that got someone upset, might be watching the death of someone in a movie; whereas trauma related sadness could actually be experiencing the death of a loved one. This puts the emotion of sadness on a large scale of numerous ways of dealing with those emotions. Of course, there's no need to assess the emotion after watching a main character die in a movie—that is just a temporary feeling that will pass almost immediately after the movie ends! What we want to really focus on is real situational sadness and even trauma. Just like anger, we need to learn how to approach and assess certain situations in order not to get stuck in them mentally. When we learn to move away from those negative emotions, and to assess those situations in the right manner, we leave room for positivity and happiness to grow within our minds, leading to nothing but success and positivity when we take the action! We need to move forward in order to move on. Living in anger and sadness will only keep us stuck in a place that will get us absolutely nowhere. This is why it is extremely crucial to handle these emotions the right way, and to move on towards a happier, healthier lifestyle.

Your thoughts are pivotal to how you operate in your daily life. What goes in is what you're going to get out in return, depending on how you handle your thoughts. As a biology major in college, I learned that the mitochondria is the powerhouse of the cell. It helps the cell to function properly and keeps it alive, and without it, the cell will die. The mitochondria produces energy for the cell, breaks down nutrients, and produces what is known as ATP, or adenosine triphosphate. This ATP that the mitochondria produces, aids in numerous functions throughout the body, such as glycolysis, which is needed to break down complex sugars so that we can supply our brains with glucose in order to go about our business every day. The mind works in the same respect. I firmly believe that the mind is the powerhouse of our body, and what you feed it is what you will produce in return. This is why it is crucial to handle these emotions that we feel almost every day, in such a way that it doesn't leave us stuck in a position in which we didn't want to be in the first place.

So, what is sadness? According to a standard definition, sadness is an emotional pain associated with feelings of loss, despair, grief, helplessness, disappointment, or sorrow. Sadness is something we all encounter as human beings, and if we don't treat the emotion in the right manner, it could lead to even bigger issues and disadvantages in life down the road. Overcoming sadness, especially trauma, can be the most difficult thing to defeat. But with the right strategies, it could be the most rewarding and self-fulfilling accomplishment in the world. All you have to do is start believing in yourself that you will overcome it, and you will. Believing is the first step to achieving, and if you don't believe in yourself, you will never make it to the next step to defeat what's eating you alive; and if you let your emotions get in the way, this would therefore lead to an unsuccessful attempt to achieve your goals. I have had so many clients in the past tell me that they couldn't do something because everything was going wrong with their lives, and they were too depressed or too upset to go through with what they loved. Remember that once you let your negative emotions override your thoughts, you are essentially giving them permission to dictate your happiness. There are plenty of people who don't go through with their goals because of a situation that happened to them months ago.

There was a guy that I knew that did not want to go through with any of his goals or what he wanted to do, because he was so caught up on a break-up that happened six months prior. He ended up going in a downward spiral, losing his job, his home, and eventually his hope. This man was unable to pick himself back up; all the hope he once had was gone after this relationship. For a while, he was in and out of places to stay, consistently asking people for money, and going to the local soup kitchen every night for a meal. He would constantly post on social media how much a failure he was, how he couldn't do anything right, and how he eventually just wanted to end it all. What this man needed was hope and motivation to get him back on the right track. With a lot of support from a few of his friends, he slowly started climbing back up the ladder of happiness and success. The first step was finding a job so that he could make an income and feed himself every day. With enough effort, and submitting application after application, he was able to find a job. Even though it was a small job that didn't pay much, it still filled his stomach every night with nourishment. A bit of hope was restored in his mind, which only led to greater results in the long run. After a few weeks had passed, he found a place to stay, with a friend, until he was able to find his own place. As the great news kept pouring into his mind and his life, so did his hope. Eventually, he was able to stand on his own two feet, and not just alone. While he was picking himself back up to get on his own two feet again, he found a new and enticing partner whom he adores very much. Currently, this man is happy and well, and I am proud to call him my friend. This man is an exemplary role model of someone with a very powerful and extraordinary mindset. I saw this man at his worst. I watched him pick himself up from the bottom of the barrel and climb to the top of the mountain, and it is all because he believed in himself first.

   This is a prime example of how trauma can ruin who we are as a person, and how we can actually lose ourselves to something that may not even be relevant five years from now. This is why it is extremely important that we recognize what we are feeling and going through, before we lose who we are and what our purpose is. Emotions and situations like this can throw us off track, and could cause us to lose our focus on our goals. This is why overcoming these emotions, and learning how to deal with them head on, is extremely important. We do not need to lose ourselves over every bad situation that happens to us in life. Fall seven times, but stand up eight. Sadness falls upon everyone. Whether it is the death of a loved one, a break-up, or a termination from a job, we cannot let sadness stop us in our tracks and let it deter us from our end goals. I knew someone who stopped doing what she loved because people kept telling her that she wasn't good enough. Once she believed that, she fell into a depression and never again did what made her happy. She let what one person said to her take truth into her mind, and she let sadness override her happiness. Never let that happen to you. Other people's opinions about you, don't matter. They don't know who you are on the inside; only you know that. They haven't been in your shoes and walked your journey before you met them, so why should you let them judge you? So before you go and do anything you love, or even if you are feeling some sort of sadness right now and don't know where to look for help, I want you to know that you are worth it, and that you can achieve anything that you set your mind to.

So how do you actually overcome sadness, depression, and anxiety? One of the first things you need to do when combating depression, is to get whatever it is or whoever it is out of your life in order to leave those toxic traits in the past. If you don't get rid of the toxic people, they will linger around, and you will never achieve the happiness you desire to have. It's like having mold in the house; if you don't remove it, you're just going to keep getting sick, and you will never get into a cleaner and healthier environment to live in. If it is a serious relationship problem, break up with them immediately. If not, talk it out. Communication is the key to maintaining a healthy relationship. You have to know where you stand in the relationship in order to make a decision. If the relationship is hurting you to the point where you are losing who you are as a person, and what you genuinely love to do, leave. The worst feeling in the world is losing who you are and leaving behind what you love to do, and if someone else is causing that, leave them. It doesn't even have to be your significant other. It could be a toxic friend or family member that is doing the damage. Whoever it is, break off contact. You need to learn how to take care of yourself and your mind first, before you can help other people.

Our mind is like a garage; we need to gutter out the clutter every now and then to make it a more spacious and healthy place to think. Imagine trying to find one thing that you remembered was in that cluttered, pain-in-the-ass garage. The next thing you know, you are tripping over stuff and falling over things you probably haven't seen in years, and most likely never even end up finding what you were looking for in the first place. In the same respect, if you don't clear your mind of all the garbage and clutter, you're constantly going to be falling upon the same issues, and making the same excuses next time around. Clean out the old garage so that the next time you are trying to find something, you could do so with ease. This makes your mind a more positive and happy place, to focus on what you need to do to become successful. A clean environment is a happy environment. When your mind is clean of all the crap and unnecessary negative thoughts, you automatically set yourself up for success.

The next step to beating depression or sadness is to feel confident in yourself, and that means in your body language as well. When you walk confidently, you feel confident. Posture and upright positions are scientifically proven to increase serotonin levels in the brain, which in turn make you feel happier and more confident. If you have ever encountered a successful person, you would probably have taken notice of their body language. They are usually walking upright in such a manner that they usually light up the room when they walk in. You would think that because of the way they look when they walk, they could be a king or queen of some country. Successful people actually do this for a reason; it actually makes them feel more confident in themselves. Try it for yourself. Stand up straight and let your chest rise just a little bit. Do you feel a tad more confident? That's because it works! Did you ever wonder why your mother always told you to sit up straight? This is why! Not only is it not good for your back if you arch it all the time, but arching your back and slouching lowers serotonin levels in the brain, making you feel the emotion of being sad. Isn't it funny how a certain posture can dramatically change your mood in an instant? Crazy, right? There was an old quote I stumbled upon awhile back that relates to this very notion: "Walk like the king, or walk like you don't care who the king is." This couldn't be more accurate. The more you walk like you are confident in yourself, the more you will be confident in yourself. The more confident you are in yourself, the more successful you will be. Get up, stand tall, and be ready to take on the world.

Remember that the world is your playground, and you only get one life, so why settle on just being average?

Another step to overcoming depression is to change your words. I will reiterate this over and over again, but changing your words is so important to how you ultimately feel about yourself. You need to train your mind to become positive, and that requires discipline. You don't know how many countless times I have heard, "I can't," or "I will never be successful because...." One of the first steps to do is to rephrase your words. Changing your attitude on how your perceive things will get you to where you have to go. Staying stuck with the same attitude all of the time will get you nowhere. But changing your attitude to a more confident and positive standpoint will take you a long way. Successful real estate investor and billionaire, Donald Trump, had a quote that always stuck with me when I needed it the most: *"Get going. Move forward. Aim high. Plan a takeoff. Don't just sit on the runway and hope someone will come along and push the airplane. It simply won't happen. Change your attitude and gain some altitude. Believe me, you'll love it up here."* I couldn't agree more with this quote. You have to change your attitude to get anywhere in life, especially if you want to be successful. No one is going to come along and do it for you; you have to do it yourself. This life is 100% your responsibility; take control of it.

Try to alleviate the depression. Take a nice warm bath with salts and soothing music. Go for a walk or focus on a hobby. You need to give your mind a rest as well, so that you don't burn yourself out mentally. This will also give you time to get your mind off whatever may be bothering you. Sometimes being occupied with a hobby, or even with work, will keep your mind on something else, and you may end up forgetting why you were even upset in the first place. Just like with anger and how I took it out on my studies, the same strategy could be applied here as well. Put your attention on something that you love doing instead—maybe your results could be rewarding! Also, get off social media as much as possible when you're upset. Looking at posts of the person you may be upset with will only make you more depressed. You don't want to post things when you are angry or upset either; this could cause the person you are angry or upset with to snap back, and it could cause greater problems than there already are. When we are angry or upset, sometimes we say things that we don't mean. So remember to stay off social media when you are not in the right mindset—it could make matters worse.

Finally, the best medicine for overcoming any sort of sadness is to talk. If you are upset about something, sometimes talking to a friend or a counselor can make a world of difference. The problem doesn't even necessarily have to be solved. Sometimes just getting it off your chest can make you feel 100% better about the situation, even to the point that it doesn't even seem to be a thing anymore. You have to let the poison out that is eating you up inside. I discussed previously about how keeping anger in is like keeping poison inside of you. The same thing goes hand in hand with depression and sadness. The more you keep it locked up inside of you, the more you will make yourself physically and mentally sick. You have to treat it and let it out; if not, it could lead to major life issues down the road, which could lead you to be unsuccessful in your endeavors. This especially applies to people with major traumas in their lives. You have to talk to someone and let it out. Once you do, you will be making way for more success to come into your life.

Chapter 4

Failure and Establishing a Winning Attitude

"The greatest glory in living lies not in never falling, but in rising every time we fall."
~ Ralph Waldo Emerson

What is failure? Failure is nothing more than a setback. Way too many people let failure control their lives. They go into doing what they love, all confident and ready to attack the next thing that comes at them, and then, bam! They encounter their first failure, get scared, pack up shop, and quit to never do what they love again. We have all heard of those stories, I'm sure. I'm also sure that you may have had an encounter like this as well. Remember that if you quit on something you said that you loved, you were never really passionate about it in the first place. So many people are scared of failure, and if you are scared of failure, then maybe you should read the chapter on fear, a second time. We all have failures at some point in life. For a child, it may be failing a test or not making the basketball team. For an adult, it may be failing at a business or not getting the job we really wanted. Everyone you talk to has failures; it's inevitable that you won't go through life without them. It is a part of life, but it's also how you deal with those failures and learn from those mistakes that really matters.

I typically use my failures as a stepping stone to motivate the heck out of me until I finally succeed at whatever I am trying to accomplish. One really hard course that I was taking in college, called Comparative Anatomy and Physiology, was a tough course that challenged me to my core. The exams we were given were really tedious and detailed, and they were about 100 questions or more in length. I would study extremely hard for these exams but only knock out B's, because of how detailed these questions really were. Sometimes the true and false section of the exam could have just a slight change in a word in the question, to determine whether the answer was correct or not. It irked me, and I really needed to get an A on that final exam. I put all of my anger into studying, and did so every day for two weeks straight, two hours a day, for that course. I knew every mechanism, every diagram, and every detail on those notes; so much so that by the end of those two weeks, I dreamt about that test in my sleep. I also watched every single YouTube video known to mankind, just to make sure I had everything down perfectly. The night before the test, I only acquired three hours of sleep, because I was so anxious to take the exam and get it over with. I walked in feeling so confident, willing to tear that exam apart with every fiber of my being. That is exactly what I did. I answered almost every single question on that exam without hesitation, except for maybe two or three questions that didn't appear to be in the notes at all. I walked out of that exam feeling so confident that I did well, and so relieved that it was over with, so that I could begin my summer vacation without any stress. That same night, I received an email from the professor that taught the class. The email read: "Congratulations,

Christine! You did fantastic on the final exam and received a 94!" I was absolutely stunned. After months of seriously studying for this course and only acquiring straight B's, except for one other exam in the beginning in which I got an A, I finally obtained the highest grade that I wanted in that course. Actually, it was higher than I wanted, but there is nothing wrong with having a higher grade! I was happy and felt satisfied with my hard work. When you go against failure with all you've got, and you never give up, you are bound to win.

Also remember that failure is never the end of the road. In most cases, you are just getting started! Think of failure as practice and a way to learn from your mistakes. If you learn a life lesson from a failure, was it really a failure to begin with? Behind every successful person lies a million other failures that the majority don't see. Do you know how many failures Donald Trump had before he became a billionaire and a hit TV star? Plenty! I guarantee you that every multi-millionaire or billionaire that you encounter will sit there and tell you about all of the failures they have had before they got to where they are today. They will also have one heck of a story! Your current situation is not your final destination. So before you think about giving up, how about giving it another try? Remember that failure isn't the end of your story; it is the beginning of your comeback story. Truman Capote once quoted: *"Failure is the condiment that gives success its flavor."* Use failure as a stepping stone to learn and grow from your mistakes, instead of sitting around and dwelling on the fact that you messed up. Mistakes are a part of life, and it's a part of how we evolve as human beings. So just because you messed up, doesn't mean that you are a mess up. Get up and try again; you only get unlimited opportunities to do so!

Many people let failure dictate how they will make their next move. They become cautious out of fear because of their last mistake. I know a lot of great business owners who did very well in their businesses throughout a good portion of their lives, but then became extremely cautious because of one major failure they had faced. They let this one failure instill fear in them for future decisions, thus carrying fear around with them, affecting every decision they make regarding their business and even in their personal lives. They tiptoe and hesitate on making decisions because of their past fiascos. Some of these great business owners, who were most likely making millions at some point, were down to only making enough to get their business by, because they were focused on taking the safe way out to save their business, rather than actually focusing on building it. I am sure that all of you probably know someone like this, or maybe it is even you. They carry this baggage of fear and failure around with them, which hinders them from actually growing and succeeding. It's like carrying a backpack of bricks around and adding a brick one by one, each brick representing a decision you make out of fear in order to take the safe way out. The bag is only going to continue to get heavier and heavier, wearing you out physically, because you have to put more physical work into your business or whatever it is that you do. It will wear you out mentally, not knowing what your next move will be to get by, or where you are headed. You will still carry around that fear of past failures and hesitations, leading you nowhere fast. It will tire you financially as well. Imagine going from a multi-million dollar business to maybe only making a quarter of a million dollars a year? A lot of people would probably have to downsize from their bigger homes, if not sell, trade in their car, or worry about what they are going to do next, because they can't afford certain things like they used to. This is all because of the fear of one past major failure. The more you carry these bricks around, the heavier they are going to get physically, mentally, and financially.

You need to clear out your mind's gutter of these past failures, and see them not as a burden that you have to live with the rest of your life, but as lessons that you learned from so that you do not make the same mistakes going forward. I'm not saying to play it the safe way to the point where you hesitate in every decision you make going forward, but just be cautious. There is nothing wrong with being cautious, but when it starts affecting your every move, it starts becoming a major problem, and that is when it is driven by fear. The more you let these fears and failures dictate your decisions, the more you are hindering yourself from further growth and success in your business and personal life. You need to take risks, and it will take money to make money. But taking risks is a part of life. I know I'd rather take a risk and have a chance of either winning or losing, than to end up with regret and say, "I wish I did this," or "I wonder what would've happened if I made this move," the rest of my life. I would rather take the risk and lose, than wind up with regret. At least if I do lose, I can learn from that mistake and use it as leverage to do better the next time around. Sometimes I even love failing more than I do winning, and a lot of you are probably thinking that I am crazy for thinking that way. But it's true. During times of failure is sometimes when the best comes out in us to do better. This is a time of prosperity when most of us get motivated to the max, because we can't stand where we are stuck anymore. Enjoying the process of the "coming up" is honestly the best feeling in the world, maybe even better than winning itself. You know that there's something great in you that is trying to become better, and you are unleashing that beast inside of you that's hungry for success. Knowing that you are striving for something better, and knowing that you are going to do better than the person you were before—beating your old self and who you were before your last failure—is the best competition you have. Also remember that you are competing against no one but yourself in this world. You will always be your greatest competition to compete against. As human beings, we are constantly evolving and growing, striving to be the best version of ourselves every day. We look in the mirror and compete against who we were yesterday, to be a better and more prosperous person today. You will always be your greatest competition; there's none that will be greater than yourself.

Sylvester Stallone came up with one of the greatest quotes, which still remains one of the best in history today. This is a quote that I genuinely live by daily, and I suggest that you do the same: *"It's not about how hard you can hit. It's about how hard you can get hit and keep moving forward. That's how winning is done."* For all of those that are carrying around the baggage of fear and past failures, know that the master has failed more times than the student has ever tried. You need to be reminded that it's not just about the decisions you make daily; it's about how you can keep moving forward despite all of the failures that you have encountered. It's about rising after the fall, and rising higher the next time around. Success comes with a multitude of failures, rejections, empty bank accounts, and people who have frequently told you "no." But none of that matters. What matters is how you kept going, and why you kept going, after the fact that you kept getting rejected. Why? Because that's how you win. Sylvester Stallone also quoted: *"Life will beat you to your knees and keep you there if you let it."* It's true. If you don't do something about those failures, you will ultimately stay stuck where you are. You see, winners never quit, and quitters never win. Those who never give up will fundamentally win in the end, while those who quit will never win at all.

Success is a result of constant failures and improvements, and without failure, we can never truly appreciate success in its fullest form. We as humans need failure in order to learn and grow. Our failures make us stronger individuals than we were yesterday. If you don't get up and fight the battle every day, you are losing to life. You have to grab life by the neck and show it who's boss. When life beats you down, you need to get back up and attack it from another level. As I always say, you are in full control of your life, so are you going to let life beat you down to your knees, or are you going to fight for what you want every day? Get up and fight the battle; you will be glad that you stuck with it. If you are ever going to be successful in life with whatever it is that you love to do, you need to establish a winning attitude. Wallowing in your sorrows about every little mistake will get you nowhere but stuck in a pit of misery. This is the reason why 99% of people don't succeed. They sulk about every poor decision they have ever made, about the news, the weather, and about whatever drama that is going on around them. They are focused so much on other people that they forget about themselves and their own self-improvement. This is why establishing and keeping a winning attitude is vital to success.

There is a mindset difference between successful people and people that choose to remain stagnant in their careers. Every successful person that has ever triumphed in their career or business doing what they love, usually always carries a positive demeanor. On the other hand, individuals that choose to remain somewhere they do not belong, and hate their careers, always seem to be so negative and futile when it comes to everything around them. Positive thinkers always tend to see the good solutions they have at hand when a conflicting situation arises; whereas negative thinkers tend to remain focused on the problem instead of searching for possible solutions on how to assess the situation. This is why optimistic thinkers generally have so much prosperity in what they do. Positivity always wins in the end. Personally, I have known so many negative thinkers that complain about where they are, but they won't do anything to fix it. They end up remaining stuck somewhere in a career that has no advantage for them in the future. It is unfortunate, because a lot of these individuals have the potential to apply themselves and do so much better. It was their mindset that was hindering them from achieving more than they were capable of. On the upside, I have also known a lot of individuals who just excelled at what they did because they had the right mindset going into the game. So many of these people continue to surprise me every day with their new ventures and achievements, and it's all because they kept a mindset of pure gold.

This is how the world separates the winners from the losers. I firmly believe that if you look towards the world with optimism and positivity, and treat others with kindness, the universe will repay you with good fortune. Whereas if you look down upon the world with pessimism and negativity, as well as being callous towards other people, the universe will pay you with misfortunes. I have seen so many negative minded people that just keep getting gifted with misfortunes, like it was some kind of curse. I have also witnessed the opposite with positive thinkers. It's like everything they touched always turned to gold. The bottom line is, be kind to the world and other people, and the world will be gracious and kind to you in return.

Developing a winning attitude generally begins with having past failures. Every major win that one experiences is usually derived from past failures. Rock bottom has built more champions than privilege ever will. Sure, there are individuals that were privileged and made it to the top, but that's very few and far between. Most of those people mainly only got there because they had their money handed to them through inheritance, or by some sort of family gift from a parent or grandparent. The 95% of individuals that made it to the top 1%, made it there by either starting their own business or putting an extreme amount of hard work into whatever it is that they love to do. Generally, these are the individuals that started at rock bottom with nothing. The famous rapper, Eminem, for example, grew up with absolutely nothing. He lived in a trailer park in Detroit, Michigan, with his mother, who had been addicted to drugs and alcohol for years. Growing up without a father figure, he was the sole provider for his mother and his little brother. Eminem worked at a car plant in Detroit, which paid very little. Every night, he would do what he loved to do, which was creating his own music. He never stopped or gave up on what he loved, for years on end. One day, he was noticed for his work, and he signed a huge record deal that made him insanely famous. Today, he is one of the world's best rappers and is worth multi-millions. He put the work in day after day, and most importantly, he loved what he was doing. Rapping was his passion, and today he is used as a prime example of someone who started from rock bottom and made it to the top—a champion.

He maintained a winning attitude despite all of the failures that he encountered throughout his life. Nothing is impossible unless you deem it that way. Also, if you want to be successful, a winning attitude just isn't enough to get you there. You must also have passion for what you do, and incorporate a ton of hard work into it. Success will never come easy; it's going to take enormous amounts of sacrifice and hard work to make the magic happen. But once it does happen, I promise you that it will be worth the wait. What always comes easy, won't last, and what always lasts, doesn't come easy. The same thing applies to success. If you take notice of the individuals that inherited their wealth, many of them are completely broke today. Why? Because they were given the money instead of given the knowledge on how to make the money. As for the individuals that started with nothing and made a success of themselves, many of them continue to prosper in what they do today. A great amount of appreciation comes into play when you are speaking of individuals that either inherit their fortunes or create them on their own. The individuals that generate their own wealth usually have a greater appreciation for their fortunes, because of all of the hard work that they put into receiving it; whereas the folks that inherit their wealth, usually go broke within six months because they don't know how to generate it.

Putting in the effort and the work is a must when you are aiming to become successful. A winning attitude just can't stand alone. You can get motivated all you want, but without action, you will get nowhere. In order to have a winning attitude, you must believe in yourself regardless of your position in life. Your economic status does not define who you are; your character does. Numerous people believe that just because they are born into a certain socioeconomic status, they will be stuck there their whole life. This simply isn't true unless you live in a country that doesn't accept capitalism. If you live in the United States, you are free to climb up and down the ladder of wealth as much as you please. You have the chance to lose all of your money, and to regain it all back and then some, with the correct tactics. Never use your socioeconomic status to deprive yourself from what you truly deserve. You are worthy of every good thing in life; you just have to show the world that you are capable of receiving it.

Excuses are a huge factor in why a lot of people that want to succeed get nowhere. They want to succeed, yet they don't want to take the action to get ahead. They use every excuse in the book for why they couldn't complete something. Such excuses include, "I don't have enough time," "I don't have enough money," and so on and so forth. If you can name it, it was probably stated at some point. If you really want to succeed in something, you will find the time and the money to do so, regardless of your current situation. Many people use excuses as a reason to stay where they are, because they are scared of change. They are scared of growing and becoming successful because they think it will make them a different person. If you were a kind person before you came into money, you will be a kind person when you receive your good fortunes. The same scenario could work vice-versa as well. If you were stingy with your money before you came into it, you will continue to be stingy when you receive it. Money doesn't change anything; it only magnifies who we were as a person before we came into it. If you seemed to become a jerk when you acquired the money, you were probably already a jerk before you obtained the money. From my own personal experience, I have learned that change is painful, but nothing is more painful than being stuck somewhere you don't belong. Change is good, and you should embrace change. You do not want to stay in a career or a place that is unfulfilling and unrewarding. You deserve to be rewarded for all the hard work that you do. C.S. Lewis quoted: *"There are far better things that lie ahead than any we leave behind."* Get rid of the excuses, and embrace change. It is only when we do that we can move forward and prosper. Excuses are part of a losing formula and not a winning one. Keep moving forward and upward.

Who we hang around with will also determine the paths we choose to go in life. Stop hanging around negative people. The more you surround yourself with negative people, the more of a losing attitude you will have, which will only contribute to further failures. If you hang out with the winners and the positive thinkers, you will notice that the conversation is completely different than when you hang with the habitual negative thinkers. Positive thinkers usually converse about goals and growth, while negative thinkers tend to focus more on gossip, drama, and what happened to Kim Kardashian four days ago. The more you hang with negative people, the more negative of a person you will become, and vice-versa if you consistently hang around the positive thinkers. Learn to remain observant, and carefully watch the actions of the people you choose to hang around. Sometimes actions speak louder than words, and hanging around those that say they do

Failure and Establishing a Winning Attitude

good things, but then do something entirely different, are things you need to watch out for and remain conscious about. Who we continue to hang around with is where we are destined to go. If you truly want to establish a winning attitude, dump your toxic negative friends and hang out with the positive crowd.

There are plenty of people who want to give up when the going gets tough. When the going gets tough, then that is when you should be buckling down even harder and going all in on what you love to do. Giving up is the attitude of a loser who was never really passionate about what they wanted to do in the first place. Social media nowadays makes everyone feel as if they are being rushed to complete their goals. If someone for heaven's sake even sees someone that they know from high school getting engaged before them, it's automatically, "OMG, JANIE GOT ENGAGED BEFORE I DID. I'LL NEVER GET MARRIED,; I'LL BE SINGLE MY WHOLE LIFE!" Yeah, whatever Nancy; if you keep telling yourself that, you just might be! A lot of people let others rush them with their timelines, and this happens with people in their career perspectives of life too, and not just in their relationship statuses. They immediately compare themselves to others instead of focusing on themselves. This could be a huge setback and a losing formula when you are trying to strive for greatness in all areas of your life. This is also a reason why people want to quit when the going gets tough, because they aren't living up to how other people they know are doing. Life is a journey, not a race. It doesn't matter how fast you get there; just get there. When your time comes, it will come. But for now, focus on yourself and stop letting other people rush you with their timelines. Also, be happy for other people; nothing good ever comes out of bitterness and jealousy.

When you give up, you are not just giving up on what you love; you are giving up on yourself. Make note of that going forward, because it is the worst feeling that you could ever experience. I'd honestly rather fail and say that I tried, than to never try at all; because if you really don't try at all, than you really did fail, big time. You need to keep pushing yourself to do better, and to strive for nothing but the best. Pain is temporary but quitting lasts forever. Never let one setback keep you back from your dreams and what you are capable of achieving. Everyone has setbacks, but it's how you come back from those setbacks that matter the most. Remember that failure is never the end of your story; it is the beginning of your comeback story. Always show up when you don't feel like showing up. It could always lead to something great, and you never want to potentially miss a great opportunity. The more you push for success, the more it will come to you. Always remember to dress up, show up, and never give up. That's the true attitude of a winner.

Chapter 5

Passion Is Priceless and So Are You

"If you do what you love, you'll never work a day in your life."
~ Marc Anthony

When do you ever really get the chance to do something you love, while creating a stream of income out of it? Most people would say never, but I am here to tell you that there are so many opportunities in this new technological era to do so! Face it, if you aren't doing what you love, and living it out in your daily career, then what are you doing? Why would you want to be stuck at a job that you hate for the rest of your life, when you could be doing what you love for a living? This is why 95% of people complain about their jobs. They aren't really passionate about what they do, and they just do it to make a living instead of creating a life. It is a very unfortunate scenario, but this is how the rest of the world thinks and lives. They want to have a stable job just to get by, while they are completely ignoring what actually makes them happy.

When I used to work at a local grocery store, not far from where I lived, I heard the complaints all of the time; not just from employees but from customers as well. I distinctly remember so many of the older folks that would come in and tell me stories about their lives and what they used to do for a living. Boy, would they complain! But this is how I learned. I always took their stories as life lessons instead of saying, "Gee, yeah, whatever pal, time to get back to 2020." I would remember how they used to complain about their jobs and all of the regrets they had for not doing other things with their lives. What hurt the most is that you could actually see the amount of pain and regret in their eyes when they would tell their stories. When they were finally finished explaining their stories, they would finish with, "Please don't let that be you." I always felt an enormous amount of sadness and pain for these people, because the regret of not doing what you love in life, can be the most painful experience you could ever face.

Even in the faces of younger individuals, you could tell that most are unhappy with what they do. Most young individuals, nowadays, only go into specific fields because of the salary it produces. Some come home every night complaining about how their day was at work, a good portion of the time. There are people that are so focused on the money that they forget about their happiness. They try to find happiness through material things, and a majority of the time, it just doesn't work out. Sadness can still lie in people that own huge mansions and fancy cars, but this all boils down to impression as well. There are a tremendous amount of individuals out there today that only want these fancy things to impress other people. Why do a lot of people really care what other people think about them? I ask myself this question every day. Throughout this generation, we have created a stigma that millions of people follow and adhere to daily. Many people concern themselves with what others will think about them if they make a decision that society doesn't like.

They let this fear emanate in the back of their minds, and instead of doing what they are happy with, they adjust to society norms accordingly. This is why some people buy these fancy things. It's not because they actually want them; it's because if you have them, it automatically makes you "cool." The real thing that makes you "cool" is your happiness, not material articles. Being happy is the real success, although 85% of people will probably not agree with me. Material items are nice to have, but if and when you do have them, be humble. Being a show-off just makes you a jerk. Remember that if you are worried about what other people are thinking about you, you are only making yourself miserable. The only opinion that matters in the end, is what you think of yourself. In all reality, if you are worried about what others think about you, those same people are probably worried about what you think about them. If you are afraid of doing something just because you are afraid of what society will think of you, you are living in fear, and you need to eradicate that immediately.

You need to do what makes you happy; it is as simple as that. If you don't, you are only holding yourself back from endless opportunities that could be waiting for you just around the bend. I ultimately believe that most people create their own unhappiness. Way too many people are caught up in drama and gossip, or they are stuck on something that was probably said to them five days ago. This is why so many people create their own unhappiness. In their minds, they live and dwell in a constant place of negativity that surrounds and impacts their everyday lives. These people therefore get used to negativity being around them, and they let it engulf them in a sea of unhappiness. Always remember that you can never change the past; you can only change the future by what you do today. Your inner world creates your outer world, and if your inner self is engorged with negative thoughts and emotions, so will your outer environment be. This is why it is extremely crucial to surround yourself with more happy and positive people; because if your inner world can create your outer world, the opposite can take adverse effects as well.

    I remember when I found out that I was truly passionate about life coaching and motivational speaking. When I was a pre-med major in college, it was definitely not an easy subject; especially while I was working a full-time job, a part-time job tutoring, and being a full-time student, all at once while trying to find study time. I was up and at it seven days a week, at five o'clock in the morning, everyday like clockwork, for a year. Needless to say, I needed some sort of motivation to get me through each day's endeavors. I would consistently listen to motivational speakers, like Gary Vaynerchuk, Tony Robbins, and Grant Cardone, through my social media feed. I became almost obsessed with listening to these great speakers and entrepreneurs day in and day out, because it's what fed my drive. It became my motivating factor to get through each and every day. Not only that, but I ended up changing my entire demeanor and who I was personally. I became more positive, inspiring, and became a person that always wanted to strive and achieve for more. I was so inspired that I even created a social media page on Facebook and Instagram, called Motivational Demeanor, to help other people get inspired as well. That's how I maintained the grades I did, and survived the work-life balance all at once.

    As a former tutor, students would always come to me for help, and sometimes it wouldn't just be about a science question. They would ask me for life advice, personal advice, career advice, and occasionally just for a little bit of motivation. Sometimes after advice was given to some of those people that I had helped, they would come back to me and thank me for all my help and advice that I had given to them just a few days prior. I became a coach. Before I knew it, I was the person that a lot of people would go to for help with a situation. It was then that I found my calling. Shortly afterward, I transferred schools, going from a community college to a four-year institution. As time passed, so did my interest in medicine. Yes, I always thought medicine was cool, but what I really fell in love with, was even cooler. People such as my family and my friends were mad at me for the decisions I was making thereafter. I decided to take an interest in seminars and self-improvement events, instead of school and grades. School became a hassle for me after my interest declined. I had no motivation to keep studying or complete homework assignments, because my heart just wasn't in it any longer. I got lectured, scolded, and even told that I was stupid for making such decisions. But what kept me going was that I constantly kept asking myself if I would be happy with doing medicine the rest of my life, or if I would be happier doing coaching and motivational speaking. A lot of people were not happy with my answer; but in the end, it's not their life, is it? It's yours.

Many of the individuals that I got lectured by, brought up the pay difference that each career path provides. Yep, money was the first thing that came to everyone's minds. Surprising, right? Well, let me ask some of those same individuals these questions. Would you be happy making $400,000 a year, doing something you hate? Or would you like to make $90,000 a year, doing something you extremely love, day in and day out? For those with a money ego, they would unfortunately go with the first choice, because it is "stable." Some people are so busy trying to make a living that they forget to actually create a life. But for those that are really passionate about what they do, they would go for the second option. This is why sadness exists in a lot of people with material assets. They chose to do something they hate for the rest of their lives, just for the money, and they only ended up with regret. On the other hand, the people that chose to go with the second option are probably living their life every day as if they were on vacation, because they are doing what they are passionate about. That is what I chose to do. I found my passion in something I originally thought I was passionate about. Coincidence, right? Heck, for the people that I do know that chose to do what they love, they are making money doing it as well, just by branding themselves. The "do what you love and the money will follow" gig is honestly true.

Also, do something you love so much that even if you keep failing at it, you will still want to get up and work hard at it every day. American comedian and actor, George Burns, once quoted, "I'd rather be a failure at something I love, than to be a success at something I hate." If you are not doing something you love, then in all reality, what are you doing? You only get a short time to live on this Earth; why spend the only life you get, doing something you hate? It never made any sense to me. I am honestly so lucky and so blessed to realize this at such a young age, while many people, unfortunately, are realizing this in their 80s, and have no way of reversing the years. I don't want you to make the same mistake as well. Today, I want you to find out what you love to do and what you are good at. It may not come right away, and that is completely fine. But do find it, because everyone has that one thing that makes them smile when they wake up in the morning. I always say that life is like picking a favorite flavor of ice cream; you never know what you are going to like best until you try them all. You might say that chocolate is your favorite flavor now, but who's to say that mint chocolate chip isn't your favorite if you've never tried it before? You have to experience. Experience is the best way to find out what you love and what you are good at. If you don't get experience, you are just going to settle for something you may end up hating in the future. Learned experience is also the best teacher, it gives you the test before it gives you the lesson. This is how people generally learn from their mistakes; you have to experience them in order to not make the same ones again.

For those that are passionate about something but are wasting their time dilly-dallying on something that is not putting them further within their endeavors, know that there is someone else out there that is trying to take that dream away from you. There will always be someone who wants to do the exact same thing as you, who is working hard, 24/7, to take your spot. Especially if you are in a very rare niche, you don't want to have to say, "Hey, he stole my idea!" I implore everyone to get a jump start on what you love to do, right away, because there will always be someone working overtime, doing what you love to do.

Many of you may also be caught between a couple of alternatives, or even stuck wondering if that one thing is ultimately what you want to do. Give that one thing another try; that is how I truly found out what I was really interested in. Remember why you started. Sometimes all it takes is a little motivation to get you back in the ring. Reminding yourself why you are on that path, can rekindle old reasons for why you chose to do something in the first place. Take a break as well. Some people lose passion for what they do because they are just downright exhausted from all of the work they have been doing to get closer to their goal. We all need to take a break at some point—after all, we are just humans! Our minds have a cut-off point that tells us, "No more, I need a break! Enough is enough!" We need to give our minds a chance to recuperate once in a while. If we don't, it could lead to a downward spiral of negative emotions and irritability, resulting in unwanted outcomes. It is quitting that leads to failure, fundamentally. There are some individuals that take such long breaks and never return to what they were doing. These are called permanent breaks. That is the point of no return. People get so comfortable being lazy that they forget about the fun in what they loved to do, prior to their so-called break. This is when most people cave in on their dreams. Do not let this be you! If you must take a break, please do so. But do not give up on your dreams; you will regret it when you are 85 and immobile! A good break can range from a few days up until a week or two. This gives you enough time to recuperate your mind and then get back to the grind. It's like taking a small vacation, except those who really do what they love, consider what they do to be an everyday vacation.

 I knew a customer that used to come into the grocery store that I worked in all of the time. He was an older man that was widowed, and his kids were distant from him. He would tell me all about his kids, his dreams, and aspirations, but then he would go into how he wished he would have done different things, and how he regretted not doing them. He would tell me all about how he wanted to be an engineer, and how he went to school but never got the chance to finish because other things in his life just got in the way. He would go on to tell me how he regretted not doing it to this day, and how he wished he could turn time around and change things. You could see the pain in this man's eyes, and not being able to physically do anything to help him, just made it even worse. This is why following your dreams isn't just a metaphor; it's a reality. If you don't chase what you love to do, you may have a rude awakening when your life is 80% over and you are wanting to turn the clock back.

Don't let your dreams be dreams—that is unfortunately the case for many people. But you are different, because you got the chance to pick up this book and read it. You drove your mindset to read this far into it and tell yourself that there is absolutely nothing in this world that is holding you back from what you love. You have to go out there and seize it. You have two choices in life: You can either sleep with your dreams, or you can wake up every day and chase them. The choice is entirely up to you. But whatever you choose, please let it be the right decision. I used to have this one teacher in high school that always told me this motto thing that made me remember him. He always told me, "Christine, MTRC." You may be wondering what MTRC stands for. It stands for, "Make the Right Choices." I could never argue with that, because a lot of decisions that I made from there on out were based on that motto. It even comes back to haunt me every once in a while, like a ghost trapped in the attic. Sometimes before I make a huge decision, it just pops in my head: MTRC. It would be so hard to forget this motto as well. Every time I would see this man, he would always repeat it, like he was trying to drill it into my head so that it would get stuck there forever. Well, it definitely worked. It stuck like a nail that was power drilled into a wall and kept there for a century. Truth be told, I have dodged a lot of bullets and bad situations that I could have gotten into, and I ended up avoiding them instead. I still thank this man today, from the bottom of my heart, because without that advice, I don't know where I would've ended up. Therefore, I want to push this motto forward to help others. I encourage you to make the right choices in whatever it may be, going forward. You never know when this motto can come in handy—MTRC.

Passion is priceless, and so are you. Having true passion for what you do, over just wanting to chase money the entire time, makes you rich in happiness. Too many people want to become successful overnight, and that just doesn't happen. Patience is a huge requirement to becoming successful, and if you don't have it, you might as well throw your dreams right out of the window. People are so focused on chasing the money rather than what they are passionate about, and that is where they fall short. They become impatient because they want a quick fix and don't really enjoy what they do. This is where 99% of people lose, because they are looking at the income portion of the spectrum, rather than focusing on what actually gets them there. Having passion for what you do is priceless. Not only do you enjoy what you are doing, but you get to enjoy the journey. The journey is what's most important, because if you don't enjoy the journey, then why continue to do what you do? Your journey makes up 90% of what is required of you to get to your destination. This is why it is pivotal to love what you do, because why would you want to go through life hating your expedition? That just means wasted years.

You only get a short time on this planet, and only one lifetime to make sure your name is in the history books; this is why you deserve to have everything that you want. Life is precious in every way possible, and it is not guaranteed every day. You have a possibility of not waking up tomorrow, so would you be satisfied with what you did yesterday and how you lived your life? Most people would answer, no! So, why are you not getting a head start on what you're passionate about now? A lot of people don't come to this realization until they are asked this question. It's unfortunate to see individuals not go through with what they love because they are wasting so much of their time on dumb stuff. This generation is being consumed so much by Netflix and social media that they don't realize how much time they are wasting on these things, instead of using it to their advantage with a multitude of opportunities at their feet. Instead of watching Netflix, how about investing in it, or using your spare time to work on your business? Instead of using social media to engage with your friends, how about becoming a social media influencer, or trying to promote your product on different platforms? There are tons of ways to turn what you love into a million dollar hit! You just have to find what is right for you. Some people do it through podcasts, while some others brand themselves and promote their product on YouTube. It all depends on what you are passionate about, and what fits into your niche perfectly. The era of the technology boom is here, and it will only soar further as advancements in technology keep growing. This means that a whole slew of new opportunities will open up in the future. But why wait for the future to bring more opportunities, when you have plenty of them at your fingertips now? It's time to stop investing your time in things that won't get you anywhere, and time to start investing in yourself and what you are passionate about. You only get one chance to do it, so just do it.

Your time is not tomorrow, and your time is not two weeks from now; your time is now, and you need to seize it. Some people wait for "the right time" to start their business or build their brand, when in all reality, there will never be a "right time." It is just an excuse to keep putting something off, because you are afraid to actually begin. Almost every excuse boils down to fear, and once we can break that fear and eliminate it completely, we will actually be able to live out our dreams to our fullest potential. Once we can acknowledge our fears and fully eradicate those thoughts, we will finally be able to become mentally free, and start living our lives as we should. Throughout your endeavors, never forget to be you. You are your best supporter and biggest fan when it comes to doing what you are passionate about. Never be afraid to be who you are throughout the process. That is the whole point of doing what you are passionate about: to be the best version of yourself and bring out who you are. You need to figure out what gets you fired up, because it is than that we can finally put what we love over monetary value. Once you are able to place what you are passionate about over anything else, and put it to work, you will open yourself up to a world of endless possibilities and a vast array of opportunities.

Chapter 6

Why You Should Be Successful

"The secret of success is learning how to use pain and pleasure instead of having pain and pleasure use you. If you do that, you're in control of your life. If you don't, life controls you."
~ Tony Robbins

There are a multitude of reasons for why you should be successful. But before we can determine why you should be successful, we need to define what success really is. There are a couple of ways of defining what it means to be successful, but that ultimately lies in the hands of the individual to determine what success is to them. What do you think of when you think of someone successful? Most people would think of fancy cars, a huge house, lots of money, and maybe even a yacht. Some may view success as quite the opposite as well. For some, success doesn't mean wealth in material things; success means having a family, great health, a good job, and just plain and utter happiness. They are two different sides of the same coin, but it's how we ultimately define success that determines where we have to go and which path we have to take. For some, happiness lies in material things, and for some others, it does not. I will also show you why material things cannot buy happiness. You can have all the money in the world and still be a miserable person. Why? Because real feelings that we have are predicated on our relationships and connections with other people, and not on our material objects.

I have seen some of the richest people, who have all the money they can possibly dream of, walk around completely angry and bitter all of the time. It didn't necessarily have to do with their wealth; mainly it had to do with something else they were dealing with deep inside of them personally. Maybe they didn't like what they were doing, or maybe they are in a marriage that's not going so well. Whatever the case may be, the riches that they had didn't make them any happier than they already were. I have also seen some people who weren't extremely wealthy but were some of the happiest people in the world, because they had their family and loved ones, which fundamentally mattered more to them than material wealth. I am not at all stating that wealth is bad, because I have seen plenty of wealthy people that are completely happy, who also donate a vast amount of money to major causes, such as leukemia and other forms of cancer, on a daily basis. There are also plenty of people without riches that walk around bitter and angry every day.

As I have stated earlier, money doesn't necessarily change who we are as a person; it only amplifies who we were prior to coming into wealth. Our happiness is based on our relationships and connections, and once we realize that, we learn that happiness is not based on material things. Of course, it is very nice to have things of luxury, and you deserve to have a mass of wealth and abundance, especially if it brings you financial freedom. But just don't think it will make you any happier than you currently are.

Why You Should Be Successful

Ultimate success should be happiness and doing what you love to do, day in and day out. That is the most pinnacle form of success: true happiness and being content with who you are and what you do.

So, why should you be successful? The bottom line is that you deserve to. Everyone deserves to be successful, because we all get the same one life that others may not get the chance to live. The chances of being conceived are slim, and the chances of actually being born are slimmer than winning the huge jackpot in the annual Powerball. Once you realize that your life is precious and unique, and that there are plenty of people who don't get the chance to become successful like you do, because they don't even have a life, this is when you recognize that you are here for a purpose that you were destined to live out. Out of the trillions of people around the world that do have life, many of them don't have the means or the physical well-being to live out their dreams, because of their government and the poor environment that they live in. Some may have the means, but they just don't know any better to realize that they have the potential, simply because nobody told them.

This is why you are considered one of the lucky ones. You live in a land of great opportunity, had the means of education, and chose to pick up this book and tell yourself that you were meant for more than just your current situation. Some of those people in those poorer countries may not have food or clean water, let alone books and education. You have all of that, plus various job opportunities, the freedom to start your own business, and internet connection right at your fingertips. You can't get any better than that! Those trillions of people I was just talking about?

You just made the cut into the few thousand! Even better, if you decide to take the action and go through with what you love to do, and make it a reality, you just made it into the very few hundred. But it is entirely up to you to take the challenge. Do you want to be successful or not? You need to believe in yourself that you will be successful. Every great thing that has ever happened to you, probably always started with having a little bit of faith in yourself. This is why you need to believe in yourself. Believe you deserve it, and the universe will serve it. You need to start by having faith in yourself that you can achieve anything you possibly desire.

The best part of becoming successful is that you can help other people become successful after you do! Leaders raise others up instead of tearing them down. Always be a leader instead of a boss; there is a big difference. Bosses command their employees and show them how things are done, while leaders help to work as a team to get things done together. Always help to make someone else a leader; the world always needs more of those! Strive to make an impact on other peoples' lives as well; that's a huge part of becoming a success. If I had the choice of making multi-millions or leaving an impact on thousands upon thousands of people, I would choose the second option, just because that would make me happy. That is the sole reason why I chose to become a life coach and motivational speaker—that and because I love to do it. I was inspired by Tony Robbins to make that dream come true. I saw the impact he made on countless numbers of people, and it inspired me to do the same. His work is truly heart touching, and I could never have found a better role model than the number one life coach in the world! Plus, I could potentially make multi-millions doing it, if I make such a large impact on those kinds of numbers of individuals.

    Throughout your mission of becoming successful, you mind is your biggest asset that you will ever have. Even in general, it is your largest, free, and most important asset you will ever have. Your largest and most important asset is a free one? You bet! You are born with a unique gift, and it is time to utilize it and take full advantage of it, because not many people do. Many people don't even realize that it is their biggest asset that they will ever have in their lives. It could lead to your success, or it could potentially lead to your downfall, based on how you put it to use. Or in the case of some people, they don't put it to use at all. No matter how young we are, no matter how old we are, we always have room for improvement to do better for ourselves. If we have the means to do it, why not do it? Greatness exists within all of us; we just have to tap into that unearthed power inside of us and ignite the flame of passion within. Your mindset and determination will get you there if you let it. You have to go out and show the world what you are made of, and what good you are capable of providing it and others around you.

    I firmly believe that your mental strength gives rise to your physical strength. Without mental strength, physical strength cannot exist, and vice versa. If you think about all of the fitness gurus that you see going down your Instagram feed daily, that essentially couldn't have happened without the help of mental strength first. What do body builders usually do when they go to the gym? They usually listen to motivational music or podcasts to get them through their workout. Either that or they go with a friend or a group of friends that egg them on to lift heavier weights. This is why doctors that tell people being diagnosed with cancer that half the battle is mental, because you need to believe it in your mind that you are feeling better, before you can go through the motions to start doing so. It's like mentally prepping for battle before you go in. You have to get in the right mindset before you are sent off to the frontline; otherwise, you can get paranoid and go AWOL, which can result in heavy consequences such as injuries or death, and maybe even a section eight. This is why PTSD arises in many soldiers. Most of us aren't mentally equipped in battle to see all of that bloodshed, which is why it is such a tough job but yet such an honor to the country.

If you have ever watched the Rocky movies, with Sylvester Stallone, you will know exactly what I am talking about. The movies are about a boxer from Philadelphia that rises to make it to the top as the ultimate heavy weight champion of the world. He begins his career as a regular old boxer that does local boxing matches in a gym. The more he climbed to the top, the harder he struggled. Some of these other opponents that he had against him were more than double his size. In the third movie, Rocky fights an opponent named Drago, a Russian boxer that was jacked up on steroids and was more than double his size. He towered over Rocky and could knock him out easily with one strike. But that didn't stop Rocky; his mind was dead set on winning that heavy weight championship. He trained for weeks on end, both physically and mentally, for his big fight with Drago, and he didn't let Drago's massive size intimidate him in the slightest. Drago may have had the bigger physical stature, but Rocky had the bigger mindset.

When it came time for the big fight, Rocky was down in the first few rounds. As time went on through the rounds, Rocky was getting pounded by this massive beast of a man. Rocky kept on and refused to be knocked out and lose his title as the heavy weight champion of the world. When the final rounds grew nearer, Rocky's trainer, Mickey, would always feed him a bunch of motivation before the end of the fight. This made Rocky fierce and ready to take home the title. No matter how many bones were broken, no matter how much blood was running down his face, and no matter how much excruciating pain he was in, he knew that belt was his. Strike after strike, he kept on clobbering Drago and moving him into the corner. Being as massive as he was, Drago wasn't used to being hit that much by an opponent. After a few more blows from Rocky's left hooks, Drago was down and unable to get up and make the count. As the saying goes, "The bigger they are, the harder they fall," and in Rocky's case, this was never truer. The bell rung, the crowd screamed, and Rocky claimed and kept his title as the heavy weight champion of the world. It was all because his mindset was bigger than Drago's physical stature itself.

This is why your mindset is so important when it comes to being successful; it is a major tool to help you win in life. Mark Twain quoted, *"It's not the size of the dog in the fight; it's the size of the fight in the dog."* These Rocky movies are a prime example of how this is definitely true. It's not about physical stature; it's about mindset. Drago was double Rocky's size, and he was on performance enhancing drugs and should've easily beaten Rocky. This proves that your mental strength and every thought you feed your mind can either build physical strength or tear it down. On the other hand, your physical strength can also feed your mental strength as well. Little comments to yourself after a workout, such as, "Yay, I did it!" or "I did really good today, but I will beat tomorrow's record!" can release a mix of hormones that create an action-reward-action cycle to boost your mental strength for the next day.

This proves that once you start feeding your mind with affirmations, such as, "I will be successful," or "I am going to be successful," and you truly and firmly believe it within your subconscious, it will start to play out in your physical life. It will become beliefs and values that you hold near and dear, and just like a culture or religion, it will start to play out in your life. Whatever goes on in the mental realm inside of your mind, causes your physical persona to function and move forward towards that thing that you subconsciously believe. This is why drug addicts, who believe that they are addicted to a certain substance, stay addicted until they go for help. They subconsciously believe in their minds that they are in fact addicted to these substances, and it causes physical dependence. That physical euphoria that one feels when addicted to a drug, tells the brain, "That felt good; let's do it again," encouraging the mental realm to feed into the physical realm yet again. It is a back and forth cycle that can either be very good for you or extremely dangerous, based on the choices you make and what you choose to feed your mind. What you subconsciously believe in your mind is what will play out as a result in the physical world. If you subconsciously believe that you are going to be successful, it will indeed carry out into your physical life.

This is why what you feed your mind is absolutely paramount to how you will spend every day of your life. The subconscious mind is a million times more powerful than the conscious mind.

This is why it is harder to break addiction patterns than most people realize, because your subconscious strongly believes that you are addicted to that drug. This is why hypnosis was introduced as a form of therapy a number of years ago, by Franz Mesmer, in 1770. He was known as the father of hypnosis. The purpose of hypnosis was to get an individual into such a deep state of relaxation, enough to get into their subconscious mind. They figured that if they could get far enough into a patient's subconscious mind, they could reverse those false affirmations that they had about themselves, and install affirmations within their subconscious, which would make them think that they were not addicted to those certain substances any longer. It usually takes more than one therapy session in order to break these patterns, but studies have shown that hypnosis does in fact work as a form of therapy. Some would also argue that it doesn't work, and that's because it may not be successful every time, depending on whether the individual is able to be hypnotized or not. Not everyone is able to be hypnotized.

This is why telling yourself you want to become successful, and actually becoming successful, fully lies on your shoulders. What you choose to believe subconsciously, sets the course for where you will go and where you will eventually end up in your endeavors. Not only do you have to fully believe that you will be successful, but you have to implement the hard work and actions daily to get there. If you truly believe that you deserve to be successful, it will happen. It may not happen overnight, because no one is an overnight success, and that's just a fact. Patience is a virtue that is required of you to get where you need to go. Setting small goals for yourself every day, and crushing them, could lead to major goals getting crushed in the long run. Little by little, small goals add up to the major goals getting done, and before you know it, time goes on, and it didn't seem like it was that long after all. It's because you are busy keeping your mind occupied and in sync with the small goals, that you don't even notice that you are getting those major goals done.

When I was in college, I noticed it all of the time. Before the semester would start, I would set myself major goals that I would want done by the end of the semester. Some of those goals would be to keep my average GPA between 3.65 and 3.8, when the end of the semester hit. Other goals would be to make sure I attained three A's and no less than one B for all of my classes, and especially to make sure that I maintained A's in my four credit classes. Smaller monthly or weekly goals would be to make sure that I got an A- on a certain exam, or a B+ on another one, just so I could maintain an average on where I stood in the class. Even smaller goals would include everyday homework assignments, reading, and studying, to make sure I was keeping up with the topics. All of those small homework assignments and quizzes that I did well on, eventually led to a good average. In turn, they led to good test and exam scores. Those test and exam scores fundamentally led to great letter scores on my transcript, which then raised my GPA even higher. The point is that the little goals getting done can snowball into the bigger ones getting completed as well, and you may not even realize it. So before you go and decide to blow off small, daily goals, remember how that can affect your larger goals in the near future.

You deserve to be successful because you deserve to be happy. As I stated in the first chapter of this book, according to Aristotle,

Why You Should Be Successful

"Achieving happiness is the highest human good." If you truly think about it, that's what everyone wants to be in the end: happy. When you only get one life to make it happen, that's when the stakes rise rapidly. That is when you begin to get a rush of motivation that tells you, "This is it; I need to do this now, because it's now or never," and that is the truth. If you don't start now, when will you start? Will you ever start? Will you waste your time significantly on nothing, like most people, and never get anything accomplished? Or will you attempt to do what you love daily until you make an impact on other people as well, and have more than you ever dreamed of? These are questions that you have to consistently ask yourself on a daily basis. Sometimes you have to stop and remind yourself of what you are doing and why you are doing it.

You are too important to not become a successful person. You are worthy of every great thing that comes your way, and you are definitely enough. You need to instill these affirmations in your mind, that you are worthy of great wealth and abundance. Once you do instill these affirmations into your subconscious, you are automatically setting yourself up for success. Every great leader once started out with these same affirmations as well. They knew they were worthy and deserved better than what their current situation had to offer them. The same thing needs to happen with you. You need to believe in yourself that you can achieve anything that you want and that nothing is impossible—that's how it all begins. Sometimes a simple belief in yourself is all it takes to go farther than you could ever imagine. Lao Tzu once quoted, *"A journey of a thousand miles begins with a single step,"* and that first step is believing in yourself.

Chapter 7

Amplify Kindness

"Once you are happy for people instead of envious, you can start the process of getting to a happy place."
~ Gary Vaynerchuk

Kindness, within the world today, is something we unfortunately don't see as often as we used to. It's something that costs nothing, yet it is something that can mean everything to someone, just based on one act of good. As I stated in the last chapter, leaders raise others up instead of tearing them down. This is why expressing kindness to others is pivotal on the road to success. Sometimes on our journey, there will be things we may not like, sacrifices we have to make, and harsh decisions we have to face going forward. People will push our buttons and antagonize us, based on who we spend the majority of our days with, and they will even try to compete with us to try and be the better person. Attaining success is not an easy task. There will be people who try to drag you down out of jealousy, but it's how you respond to them and what you decide to do that determines whether you make the world a better place or you decide to play along with their shenanigans.

There will be friends that leave you because you don't spend every second with them, because you're using that time to work on your goals. There will be friends, family members, and significant others that will turn on you, especially when you need them the most. We sometimes have to make what's known as sacrifices, so that we can improve ourselves every day in the long term. Maybe, for you, it's sacrificing seeing your kids basketball game, to stay later at the office in order to provide for your family. Maybe it's paying a loan that you've been holding off on, instead of buying that brand new car. Whatever it may be, there will be things in this world that disgust you, and people that will try to bring you down to their level to accompany them, but it's how you respond to the world that matters the most. Most people respond with anger and would take it out on everything and anyone near them.

In Chapter 3, we learned how anger is a weak emotion, and I expressed different ways of overcoming it. If you feel angry towards someone that has either criticized you or did you wrong, you are allowing what they said or did to affect you emotionally. You are fundamentally giving what they said or did, permission to hurt you. I also quoted Nelson Mandela: *"Resentment is like drinking poison and expecting it to kill your enemy."* Being angry is basically like drinking poison that your enemy had given you to drink, and expecting it to kill them. But this is normally the way that most people respond to criticism or any other type of situation that is not in their favor. I will also show you how to combat scenarios like this with kindness. Now kindness isn't the first emotion you feel like expressing after someone has just criticized you, but when you combat hate with kindness, you systematically open yourself up to a whole new world of freedom and happiness.

Kindness is mistaken as a weakness almost all of the time by other people. But in all reality, spreading kindness in the face of hate is what makes you stronger. The people who generally mistake kindness for weakness usually face hate with bitterness or anger, which are all weak emotions. So kindness is usually mistaken as a weakness by weak people? Go figure. It happens all of the time, every day, 24/7. Some people think that just because you don't respond to their criticism with anger, that you fear them in some sort of way, or that you are vulnerable and they must have gotten to you; when in all reality, that is not the case at all. I have a task for you. The next time someone criticizes you or does something to try and make you angry, don't get angry. I want you to keep on smiling and say, "I forgive you, and if you ever need me, I am here to talk. By the way, I like your shoes." This will make them think for a little bit. But fighting hate with kindness is the strongest thing you can do. If they keep antagonizing you, let them go. They just won't get what the whole point of that statement was. Also, actually forgive them in your heart. It is the only way to let go of poison and move on. You need to fight pessimism with optimism; it's the only way to try and make this world that we live in a better place. This will also help you to improve as a person on the road to true happiness and success.

We also need to realize that other people have pain and troubles too. So before you judge anyone, make sure you know what is going on in their lives, and know their whole background story. This is honestly why we shouldn't judge anyone at all. We won't know every detail that goes on in their lives unless they decide to tell us. If you don't want others judging you, you shouldn't be judging them either. Throughout my journey as a life coach, I post videos to my social media pages as well, to try and get my messages across. In a lot of my videos, you will hear me go on about how we live in a judgement-filled society. I also explain how we should stop living in a judgement-filled society, and start living in a judgement-free society. Living in a judgement-free society today is nearly impossible. But when you strive to make an impact on other people, hopefully that message gets conveyed across to someone else, and they pass on the torch as well. This is why we have to convey our messages as much as we can while we have the opportunities, such as with social media, books, cell phones, and the internet. If you have a message for the world, it is so much easier to transmit now than ever before. Pass on the torch of kindness, and stop letting yourself live in a world full of judgements. Stop caring about what other people think of you, and just be kind.

Spreading kindness and making it louder, in a society that has lost its ways and values, can possibly create a ripple effect someday, causing it to find some sort of way back into mainstream society. Even making small, random acts of kindness like opening the door for someone behind you, or paying for the person in front of you at the drive-thru every once in a while, can honestly make someone's day or cause an effect. Maybe that same person will do something nice for someone else in the near future. Kindness costs zero dollars, so why shouldn't we pay it forward every day? The cold hard fact is that we don't. Society has become so bitter and stuck in their angry ways that they have forgotten what it's like to be compassionate every now and then. With the consistent arguing between politics and media, and the shootings and mass murders in the daily news, the world has lost touch of any sense of love and compassion. I bet if you turn on the news station right now, nine out of ten times it will either be something that saddens you or angers you. There are rarely ever any hero or good guy stories in the media anymore. If you go outside, you will even notice that people are mainly grumpy and complaining about whatever it is that may be going on in their lives. This is why we need to amplify kindness. We have to claim it back as a part of society, and who we are as an individual person as well. We need to show the world that we are not all bad people.

The unfortunate part of all of this is that you are always made out to be the villain in someone's story. No one will ever have a perfect image, and that's what makes us human. No one is perfect, but everyone is capable of showing kindness. One random act of kindness that you did a year ago could have meant the world to somebody, and you may not even know it. There will also be times, or there may have already been times, where you have been nice to people that didn't appreciate it. Never regret being a good person to the wrong people. Your kindness says everything about you, and their behaviors say everything about them. Never let that affect you to the point where you stop being kind to others, and become cold to the world. That's how you lose your touch as a person, and it could lead to losing who you are at the same time. Some people just show their true colors through their behaviors, and you don't need that kind of negativity to bring you down as a person. You need to cut the toxic people and behaviors out of your life, before it becomes poisonous to your persona. If you don't cut out the toxins that are harming you, it could affect you on your trek to success. Never stop being nice, because being kind is what makes you a better person inside and out.

There are always those people that have made it and have been very successful in their careers or business, who just feel too important to be nice to people. They let their ego decide for them if they should be nice or not, because they feel entitled that they shouldn't have to be. These kinds of people let the material things go to their head. But as I have stated in earlier chapters, money just magnifies who we are as a person. So, whoever feels entitled that they shouldn't be nice, based on their status, probably was a bitter person back then too. Having a sense of entitlement is honestly the worst thing that is happening within this generation currently. Many of these young kids feel entitled that they don't have to work or pay bills, because they think that they are too good to get their hands dirty.

The sad part is that most children are being brought up this way with a false sense of entitlement, which is given to them by their parents. This sense of entitlement that these children think that they are permitted to, creates an ego that only leads to destruction further down the road. As they go through life with this sense of entitlement, they start to believe that they are too good to do certain tasks that get their hands dirty, or they start looking down on other people of lower class, because they were raised and taught that having a job, such as a janitor, would be considered a disgusting career. They then have this image produced in their head that they are too good to have a job like that, and will never even think about cleaning bathrooms to make money. This also leads to feelings of bitterness and anger as these children grow older, and it robs the thoughts of kindness and compassion right from their minds. Once they grow up as successful and accomplished adults, they start to feel as if they are too important to be nice to people. Partially, it's because their parents instilled in them degrading thoughts of lower-class people, instead of showing them that it doesn't matter what you do for work, as long as you provide for your family and put food on the table. You are never too important to be nice to people. In the end, if you are really successful and still treat someone else with disrespect, you don't gain anything at all, except to be a jerk with a false sense of entitlement. If you have seen that most multi-millionaires treat people with the utmost kindness and respect, it is because they know what it's like to start from the bottom and work themselves all the way up to the top. When they get to the top, most of them hold their hands out to help others up as well. Leaders raise other leaders up instead of tearing them down.

Treat others with the same respect that you would want. You wouldn't like it if someone criticized your hard work, would you? We get nowhere by degrading people and spewing hate and bitterness. But we can get somewhere by working together and spreading kindness and compassion. Even when you think you know everything, you don't. When you do become successful, don't think you are the smartest person in the room either. We learn and grow every day, and I love to continue to learn new things on a daily basis. There is always room for growth and improvement in our daily lives. Those who think that they are the smartest person in the room, are inevitably in the wrong room. There are people that do think that they are smarter than everyone else, and that is actually a downfall of their own persona. I am sure you at least know one person that thinks that they are God, and heaven forbid you tell them that they are wrong. This is also what is known as the Dunning-Kruger effect. It is a cognitive bias in which people assess their cognitive ability to be greater than it actually is. They have an inability to recognize their lack of ability, due to a severe false conception of superiority.

If you think that you are smarter than anyone else, you are limiting your learning capabilities severely. You become resistant to new information that is thrown at you every day, because you try and swat it away to try and prove somebody else wrong. You can state your case that you were right all you want, when in reality you probably haven't even heard what the theory was in the first place. We need to acknowledge and assess our downfalls, instead of suppressing them with false affirmations about ourselves. Use your vulnerabilities to your advantage, and utilize them to make you a better and stronger human being. Turn the negative attributes about yourself into positive ones, and strengthen your downfalls wherever you see fit. The moment we can admit when we are wrong, is the moment where we can step up to the plate in every other situation, with confidence. Once you master correcting the faults within yourself, you set yourself up for exponential success. That's also how you learn and earn respect. Absolutely no one likes a know-it-all. Learn to admit when you are wrong; that's how you gain strength within yourself. In all honesty, if you want to be smarter, hang out with people that are smarter than you. This will only propel you to become more successful in the future! These are the scenarios that unfold when you choose to open up your mind, instead of remaining stagnant and closed-minded because of an ego issue. When you are willing to realize that there are people out there better than you, you suddenly become willing to learn more and to improve yourself in the process.

I had a friend a while back that used to think that he was smarter than every other light bulb in a hardware store. He would even consistently state that he was smarter than everyone else he knew. But when you would listen to this guy talk, he would contradict himself on every other level. Of course, he had an ego problem. But I felt bad for him; I was wondering if he knew of his own deposition. This guy would also degrade other people for their lower-class status in society. I felt bad for him that he could not see the flaws in himself because he thought he was so superior to everyone else. No matter who you are, we are all human beings at the end of the day. We all have faults, we all make mistakes, and we all don't have a perfect image like society wants us to. But we need to admit when we are wrong, and fix our mistakes. There is a reason why pencils have an eraser, because no matter who is writing with the pencil, we all are going to make a mistake that we are going to have to admit and fix at some point.

Kindness is the catalyst that propels and makes our personalities more constructive. A lot of people see kindness as a weakness in business, only because many people stereotype business owners and top CEOs as stern and tough people, who won't back down until they get what they want. The last part of that is true, but the first part of that is not always the case. I myself know plenty of down-to-earth and kindhearted business owners who are very successful in what they do. In business, having a kind personality could set a great foundation with business partners and affiliates, thus establishing trust and forming fulfilling relationships. This can cause business to do very well when relationships are running smooth. It takes a long time to build trust, and just seconds to break it; this is why forming relationships based on kindness, instead of bitterness, is crucial. Building business relationships based on bitterness, can lead to suspicion and weariness of your business affiliates, instead of trust. This can cause arguments and can even damage profits and how much revenue you bring in. Let's face it; if your business affiliate was suspicious of your business endeavors, would he or she want to work with you or pay you what they think you deserve in the deal? I don't think so. Building your relationships based on kindness, confirms trust and reduces weariness of your business endeavors. This assembles a great deal of trust between you and your business affiliate, thus most likely increasing the profit into your establishment.

    There will also be people that try and manipulate you for your kindness because they view it as a vulnerability that you have, instead of a strength. This might lead to situations such as getting robbed out of a deal or not getting paid what you deserved to be paid. While you want to remain a kind person, you also want to show these kinds of people that you are tough and strong too, and that you won't back down until you get what you deserve. You want to remain kind, but you also want to remain steadfast and diligent in your work. Don't ever take it overboard to the point where you seem like a complete jerk that scrutinizes everyone if you don't get what you want. The reason you want to remain tough is because you don't want people to manipulate your feelings. People will see your kindness as an opportunity to prey on someone they see as a feeble individual, and try to screw you out of a deal. If you choose to remain centered, grounded, and calm, as well as providing a kind but yet stern atmosphere, you are setting yourself up for success.

A lot of my inspiration from this chapter comes from a very successful and well-known man all over social media. Gary Vaynerchuk opened my eyes and showed me what it is like to spread kindness, and how we need to harness it to be successful ourselves. He always states that nice guys always win in the end, and bad guys, posing as the good guys, always lose. You can't argue with that theory, because it is completely true. Kindness conquers all. Vaynerchuk has been a huge role model for me in my career as a life coach and motivational speaker. I have learned so many great things from his wisdom, and ultimately changed and transformed my life because of him. I am very thankful for his genuine love for his fans, and his love for his high-quality content. My goal is to continue to spread love and kindness amongst a generation that is in need of it most, and I hope you can continue to do the same.

Reacting with kindness instead of pungency is always the right thing to do. No matter how much someone is trying to make you angry or to manipulate your feelings, you have to kill with kindness and stand strong. This world is a brutal place, and if you don't stand up for what you believe in and what you know is right, it will take you down with its bare hands, bone for bone. Kindness is your weapon, and anger and futility is your enemy. You must kill hate with kindness, and raise up other leaders to help you in your pursuit. This world needs to be won back with kindness and compassion, and desecrated of all anger and exasperation. We need to show the world that nothing is impossible once we show a single face of kindness among a sea of sameness and malevolence. Kindness must rise to its feet and radiate warmth, just as the sun rises and shines every day. We must rise to the challenge and lend a helping hand to others, for if we do that, it is then that we can truly become successful ourselves.

Kindness conquers all wrath and outrage in the end. No longer will hate and indignation fill our souls and cause discontent by choice. It's time to choose kindness over bitterness, compassion above hostility, and adopt love over hate. We must stand up for ourselves and take a shot in the dark to fight for our triumphs. Hope must be kept alive, like a flame that flickers off in the distance. We need to ignite the flame of passion within ourselves, and never burn out the energy that keeps it extant. Let it continue to grow and spread like the happiness upon a child's face. Allow it to bring warmth to who you are, and let it expel upon the earth so that others may feel its warmth as well. Live to leave your footprints upon thousands of hearts across many generations, for it is not what we create but what we leave behind that is a reminder for future posterity. Leave a legacy that will never be forgotten, and a spirit of energy that sparks the flame of enthusiasm in children all over the world. Broaden hope, disperse love, and overall, amplify kindness.

Chapter 8

Energy, Momentum, and Discipline

"If you get up in the morning and think the future is going to be better, it is a bright day. Otherwise, it's not."
~ Elon Musk

Have you ever woken up in the morning and dreaded getting up because you wanted to sleep in, instead of going to work? I am sure we all have had those days. Even I feel the same way every now and again. Energy is important when you are aiming to become successful. If you take notice of the great entrepreneurs, such as Tony Robbins and Donald Trump, you'll realize that they only usually sleep 3-4 hours a night. Some people may think that it's insane, because science normally suggests that the average adult get eight hours of sleep per night. But for Tony Robbins, he can't wait to wake up in the morning. Four hours is sometimes all he needs to function to his fullest extent the next day. He thinks it is absolutely vital to experience every hour of life that you have. I honestly couldn't argue with that. He also states that it is his passion that wakes him up in the morning, and that he wakes up naturally, without the aid of an alarm clock. Going to bed late and waking up early is a daily trend for entrepreneurs and for people that value their passion more than their sleeping habits. Many people would ask, where do these people get the energy to do this every day? It's simple. Your passion is the fuel that provides the car with energy to get it where it needs to go. If you're not truly passionate about whatever it is that you do, you will never experience that true energy.

Going to bed late and waking up early, every single day, is an exhilarating experience like no other. As a student, before I currently did what I do now, I would wake up at 5 A.M., 7 days a week, and either go to work or school, and by the time my day would end at around 7 P.M., I would go home and work on homework and study until eleven at night, only to wake up and do it again the next morning. But I loved what I did, and I never had a day off to myself for about a year, unless I had a holiday break. But even then, I would be busy working on something else. It became second nature to me, and I learned to love the hustle. You have to have passion for what you do, because passion is what drives your energy to function through your daily tasks. My family almost never saw me, unless it was time for dinner or to see me off in the morning for a brief few minutes before work or class. When I would put in a request for a day off, even for my birthday or something special, they'd say, "Oh my gosh, when do we ever get the chance to see you and actually hang out with you? You're either always working, at school, or studying. We never see you anymore." It was completely true. Between the ages of 20 and 21, I had worked myself to death. That's why any day that I did get off to spend with my family, they treated it as if it were extremely special. Over the last couple of years, things have slowed because of my transfer and then my career change. But I am still working hard every day on what I love to do, and I couldn't be happier.

This is why having energy is so important; your energy not only drives what you do, but it drives your personality and daily attitude as well. Having a good form of energy flow through your system can cause you to be happier and to stay on top of things; whereas having your energy thrown off once in a while, can place you in a bad mood and cause things to get choppy within your daily routine. Have you ever been around someone and felt good or bad "vibes?" What you are feeling is fundamentally someone else's energy. You need to trust this intuition as well. Who you hang around daily can also build the energy around you. If you are consistently around negative people, negative energy is bound to form around you; whereas if you hang around like-minded, positive people, with the same goals as you, it could only emanate positive energy from there. Who you choose to hang around with, in the long run, will determine your path in life. This is why it is pivotal to choose your friends wisely; they represent who you are. Choose to hang out with people who will be a good influence on your life instead of a negative one.

You have to wake up and tell yourself that it is going to be a great day, instead of dreading to get up in the morning. Once you do this, you are rewiring your subconscious to say that you are dead set on having a great day, no matter how many odds are against you. You are essentially welcoming good energy and vibrations to flow in your favor. This is why it is important that you consistently tell yourself positive things. When you do, you are allowing positive energy to flow in your direction as well. Your energy ultimately affects the people around you and who you end up inspiring. People can feel your energy. I'm sure you've probably encountered someone that has been in a really bad mood and has walked past you as if they didn't want to talk to anyone. Maybe it didn't even have to do with you; maybe there was something going on in some other aspect of their life. I'm also sure you've encountered the opposite as well. Maybe someone walked into work in the morning, excited and dancing around because they just found out that they got a promotion. You'd probably ask, "What's with them?" Am I right? The same thing can work in respect to the negative attitude as well. The attitude sets the tone in the atmosphere as well; it's the energy one throws off. I'm sure that when you experienced someone else's great, grand attitude, you thought, "Wow, I like his attitude; it feels good." You may not realize it, but your energy affects those around you too. If your goal is to inspire, you want to give off that positive energy in the atmosphere. When you ultimately feel good, you do good as well, and it affects everyone else around you too, based on your energy. When I took a course in psychology awhile back, this was known as the feel-good, do-good phenomenon. Have you ever just found out that you received an A on a test, and suddenly you just found yourself in a great mood, wanting to help other people as a result? That is what is known in psychology as the feel-good, do-good phenomenon. This can work in the opposite respect too. Have you ever noticed your mood when you flunked a test? You probably didn't want to talk to anybody, or do anything to help them, am I correct? This probably gave off bad energy to those around you, and caused them to feel a little alarmed too. This is why the energy you give off is vital if you want to encourage a more positive atmosphere. Realize that your energy just doesn't affect you; it also affects those around you.

Energy, Momentum, and Discipline

Your energy is what can either make you or break you. If you start out with negative energy in the morning, you will most likely have a bad day, unless you decide to do something that changes your attitude. Having consistent negative energy can cause a great deal of issues, especially when you are trying to become successful. This can place you in a bad mood and cause all of those negative emotions to spiral into your life and do damage. This is why it is crucial to keep positive energy flowing into your life, on your end and from those you choose to have in your life. Having that positive adrenaline rush is always the best feeling, and it will almost always lead to great things if you let it. It's time we stop sleeping in late, and start waking up early to work on our dreams. Just think about it; the more you sleep in, the more time you are wasting and not getting your goals completed. There will always be someone else trying to do exactly what you want to do. They are waking up early and going to bed late every day, to crush their goals while you continue to sleep on yours. One day, all your hard work, late nights, and early mornings will pay off, and you will finally be able to say that you made it. But right now, you have to put the hard work and energy in, simply because no one is going to do it for you. Continue to allow positive energy into your life, and allow it to radiate out to others' lives as well. It will require tons of hard work, sacrifice, energy, consistency, and stamina to get where you want to go, and it won't be easy. But once all is said and done, it will be worth all of the hard work and suffering that it took to get there; which takes us to the next topic—momentum.

Sometimes momentum can be the difference between winning and losing. Momentum is getting up day after day without hesitation to work on your goals. Taking frequent breaks on your goals can cause a huge backup, and you can lose time while doing so in the process. This is why momentum is a leader's best friend. The moment you stop, you're automatically setting yourself up for failure. Getting started is the hardest part to gaining momentum and getting the ball rolling. It takes a lot of work to start a business, or to create a YouTube channel that you want to do well and make money on. It is going to take a multitude of blood, sweat, and tears, but once you get started and keep going, your success rate is inevitable. In physics, you learn that an object that is at rest, stays at rest. Objects in motion tend to stay in motion, unless acted upon by an outside force. When objects are in motion, and stay in motion, that is what is known as momentum. Those who decide to sit on the couch and flip channels all day, will most likely be in the same position six months from now if they don't make a life altering decision quickly. If you take a look at great CEOs and entrepreneurs, they are all over the place and always on to the next thing. Usually they take on one task right after the other, and you wonder when they even get a chance to breathe. But this is why they are as successful as they are. They keep putting their hard work and sweat into everyday goals and tasks without complaint, and the people that are flipping channels usually just call them lucky for all of the money they have. These are also the people that wonder why they are always broke, because they don't go out and do anything about it.

    Momentum doesn't have an on and off switch. You can't just start something such as a business and get it halfway running, only to desert it for a few weeks and decide to come back to it later. Your business will ultimately fail. This is why momentum is an entrepreneur's best friend. Momentum is not a start-and-stop process; it is a "go" process, all the way down the racetrack. Imagine if your heart didn't have any momentum. Your heart usually beats 80 beats per minute, 24/7, for the rest of your life. What if it were to stop? That would be what is known as a myocardial infarction or a heart attack, and you would die in an instant. This is why the stop-and-start method will not work in business or whatever career you are in. The moment you stop is the moment you sink. This is why, every moment, you have to keep momentum. The key to getting started is to take one step at a time and work your way up from there. The hardest part is always taking the first step, but that is also half the battle. The other part of the battle is to keep it going; because if you stop, you may not ever have the motivation to get going again. If you do, you would just have to start the process all over again, and that would just turn into a hassle. The death of momentum, leads to the death of your goals.

In order to keep momentum, you need to keep up your motivation levels. Your motivation levels are what keeps you motivated towards doing what you love, which only leads to massive success in turning your dreams into a reality. This is why your mindset and what you choose to feed your mind is crucial. One thing snowballs into another, and it all begins with your mindset and a vision. The goal is not only to get motivated but to also stay motivated. Staying motivated is the key to keep your momentum rolling forward. Once you know what your vision is set up to look like, and you get your motivation levels all set to go, ask yourself what your first step will be in order to gain momentum. In order to build momentum, you first have to have a plan in place on where you will be headed. You want to have a strategy towards your goals. You don't want to run around aimlessly, like a chicken with its head cut off, because you are confused on where to go next. Ask yourself, "Where am I going from here?" It will make the process easier and more efficient on your end. Slow breaths, small steps, and having a strategy are important. You want a clear grasp on what you are doing and where you will be going next. This makes it much easier to navigate through the processes and get your goals accomplished even faster and more efficiently. Take one step at a time, and focus on one task at a time. Focusing on too many things at once can get confusing and just be downright frustrating, which could even cause you to lose ambition. This is why it is important to take things slowly at first. You don't want to set yourself up for potential mistakes by starting out too fast and not knowing what you are doing. But once you get the ball rolling, be persistent. You don't want to stop all at once and lose time towards achieving your goals.

I live by a method that I call the 3 P's of success: positivity, persistence, and patience. The number one P is positivity, because you always have to start with having a positive mindset. If you don't start with a positive mindset going into what you are doing, you are automatically setting yourself up for failure. As I have stated repeatedly, your mindset is the biggest asset that you have, and if you feed it garbage and negative thoughts, then that is what you will get out as a result. The second P of success is persistence, and this is where momentum swings in to help you get you closer to your dreams. You need to be persistent in what you do, because if you stop, you are going to get nowhere, except to wonder why you ever stopped in the first place. If you stop your momentum, you are delaying your goals and pushing your dreams off even

Energy, Momentum, and Discipline

farther into the distance. Persistence is like the space in between a key and a lock. You have to use your energy to place the key in the lock, to open the door to your dreams. You have to keep doing this multiple times, different ways, in order to achieve all of your goals. The key represents all of your ambitions, hopes, and dreams. Also on that key are the certain ridges in the way it is structured, which unlock certain doors to your destiny. Those ridges represent the different strategies you will use in order to achieve those specific goals; whereas the lock is the obstacle that stands between you and your goals. You have to use the specific strategies on those keys to unlock certain aspects of your aspirations. Persistence is just the thing that gets you there. You have to keep using and trying different keys to eventually unlock your destiny. That is your momentum. The moral of the story is to never give up. Finally, the third P of success is called patience. As I have stated before, no one is an overnight success. It's going to take time. But when it finally happens, you will be happy, and it will be worth the wait.

Use your energy and put it into your first step. After that, put it into your second, and so on and so forth, until you really start picking up the pace on building momentum. This is the secret to getting to your goals a lot quicker and more efficiently. Energy and momentum coincide with each other, and work with one another, much like a baseball fits to a baseball glove. You need one just as much as you need the other, and they cannot exist without each other in the long run. You can have energy, but it is nothing without momentum. You will have nothing to put that energy into, rendering it useless. Momentum works in the same respect. You cannot have momentum if you do not have the energy. Energy is what puts momentum into motion so that you can get things done. But all of this is essentially useless if you do not keep on top of your goals every day, seven days a week, like clockwork. This is why you need to train your mind to be disciplined.

    You can have all of the motivation, energy, positive attitude, and momentum that you want, but without discipline, it could all go to waste in no time. The most successful people in life are disciplined. Disciplined people are not satisfied with living just an average life. They train their mindset in such a way that they can be successful in what they do. When you are disciplined, you aren't out partying every day while letting your goals sit there in the dust, just for you to come back two weeks later and work on them. Disciplined people work hard all day every day, sacrificing hangouts with their friends and family so that they can achieve their goals in a timely manner. Part of becoming successful also means disappearing for a while. Sometimes you need to be on your own in order to get a good portion of your goals accomplished. This means giving up things that ordinary people might do daily. Sometimes it's best to stay off Netflix, stay out of the clubs, and to stay laser focused on your objectives, if you want to be successful. If you were to ask a bunch of multi-millionaires how much they watched television, I bet they would tell you that it would be slim to none. Why do you think that you have never seen a Lamborghini commercial on TV? Because the people who can afford them aren't sitting around watching television. Lamborghini knows that they won't reach their target market that way, because most of their customers that can afford them aren't couch potatoes.

    The people that aim to be successful usually outwork anyone

else, because they are so dedicated to their dreams. It's their vision and passion that keeps them motivated to stay disciplined on their work. This is the main reason that they are successful. They see something that they want, and they don't stop until they get it. This is the kind of attitude that you need to have for your dreams if you want to be successful in what you do. Having a disciplined mindset causes you to stay on top of your tasks, and to keep on track with your goals. When your mind is not disciplined towards your work, you will fall through on your responsibilities, and you will eventually fall behind on your success as well. This is why it is important to keep your mind disciplined. You don't want to fall behind on achieving your goals; this will only amount to wasted time and upset in the end. If you are really passionate about what you do, you should have no problem keeping a disciplined mindset. It all comes down to what you value more in the end. There are plenty of successful people who have struggled with drug addictions in their lives, before they were ever successful. One day, they just decided what they valued more of in their lives, instead of what brought them down. For some, it was asking the question: "Should I choose the drugs or the greatness inside of me that I am capable of becoming?" Luckily for most, it was choosing to unleash the greatness inside of them, and to experience their true potential.

It is important to love what you do, because this makes it a million times easier to stay disciplined and focused on your goals. Once you know exactly what you want, and you just go for it, it makes having the energy, momentum, and discipline a lot easier than if you are unsure. Disciplined people grow the most when they are frustrated, because most successful people like to take on new challenges. Here they stay open-minded and try to test what they could take on by accepting these challenges. When disciplined people are challenged, their problem-solving skills are called upon, and this is where they are truly tested on their levels of commitment to their targets. Discipline comes when you are truly dedicated to stay committed to your goals. When you are truly committed, discipline should be no problem. It's easy to be motivated when everything is going well, but the goal is to stay disciplined when the going gets tough. Self-discipline is one of the major keys to great success in life. Without it, there is no chance of success. You have to remain extremely dedicated. Self-discipline helps you to become unstoppable, unleashing your energy to reach the greatest levels of success in your life.

Training your mind to become disciplined creates habits, and habits form who we are and where we go in life. The 21/90 rule states that is takes 21 days to either make or break a habit, and 90 days to create a lifestyle. This is a great rule to live by, because if you want to make healthier and better life choices for yourself, getting into the habit of actually doing these tasks every day can instill them in your mind, which then turns them into a habit that ultimately disciplines your mind to make better choices, day in and day out. In psychology, this is also known as classical conditioning. You are selectively conditioning your mind to choose a better lifestyle based on your habits. This can also work in a negative way as well. For example, if you smell someone cooking a certain kind of food that you do not like, you may have a certain aversion to that smell. Your mind is conditioned to hate the smell, simply because you associate that with the taste of the food itself. This is why it is important to form good habits, because you can essentially condition your mind to form certain habits very easily. Do you ever wonder how nutritionists stay on a healthy diet and barely ever crave junk food? It's because they have conditioned their minds to do so. I'm sure, in the beginning, it is very hard not to crave the delicious sweets. But the more you discipline yourself and condition your mind, the easier it gets. The more you turn those healthier choices into a habit, the more you can get things done.

Disciplining your mind also helps you to keep focused on tasks at hand. Successful people usually have laser sharp focus when they have specific objectives they want to fulfill. Honing in on your targets, and knowing exactly what you want to get accomplished, also builds momentum and helps you to achieve your goals. Discipline helps you to stay focused and build up your work ethic. This in turn can also boost your self-esteem. Once you realize that you are achieving your goals, it can boost your sense of self-esteem, causing you to increase your work ethic as a result. This also feeds into the action-reward-action system that was mentioned earlier. The more hard work and action that you place into your goals, the more of a positive reward you will get in return, substantially creating a sense of motivation to do even better come your next task. If you keep working on your goals, but you seem to be either getting nowhere or just completely failing at them, this is where having a winning attitude is crucial. Remember that failure is only a setback, and that the only way you can ever really fail is to not try at all. You only ever fail if you stop trying. Remember that behind every successful person lies a multitude of failures. Also, if something doesn't seem to be working out in your favor, try a different strategy or method. It never will hurt you to try new things, and old ways won't open new doors. Be open to new strategies and new possibilities as well. You can't expect to succeed just by using the same strategy over and over again. Different strategies work for different things. Success comes to those who believe in themselves, and the key is to put massive amounts of hard work into doing what you love. Always strive to be the hardest worker in the room, because that will ultimately set you up to be a successful person.

Discipline also helps you achieve mastery in what you do. Success doesn't come to beginners; it comes to those who truly master the art of what they do. This also shows why being self-disciplined is absolutely pivotal to your success. You need to get into the habit of putting in the work 24/7, 7 days a week, in order to become a master at what you do. Success doesn't come to those who consistently party every weekend; it comes to those who stay disciplined and work on the weekends while everyone else is out partying. This is what separates the 99% from the 1%, the bottom crowd from those at the top. If you want to be in the 1%, you have to do the things that the other 99% aren't willing to do. You have to suffer through the work now, and make sacrifices in order to live out the rest of your life as a champion. You have to remain dedicated, disciplined, and focused while everyone else is focused on binging Netflix series, drinking, and partying. What kills me is when unsuccessful people tell successful people that they just got "lucky." They aren't lucky; they just worked for something that you didn't. It isn't the status you were born into that determines your financial wealth fifteen years from now; it's your choices.

You may be born poor, but you have the choice of not staying where you are if you don't want to. There are plenty of opportunities out there to improve yourself financially; you just have to go out there and search for them. The opposite can happen as well. You can be born into a rich family but end up impoverished based on the choices that you make. There are plenty of famous and wealthy individuals today that started out dirt poor; it was their choices that got them to where they are currently. But if you want to truly be successful, you have to remain disciplined. It's the only way to the top. When you remain disciplined, not only can you master what you do, but you can bring out the best version of yourself that you didn't even know existed. Success is no accident. Success comes to those who truly deserve it, and if you want to truly be successful, then you have to change your outlook on life and your current work ethic. You have to become the best version of yourself in order to succeed in life, and this means being willing to improve yourself on a daily basis. When you do something consistently day after day, you will only become better at it. This is what makes discipline a vital part of success.

Chapter 9

Glorifying Gratitude

"As we express our gratitude, we must never forget that the highest appreciation is not to utter words, but to live by them."
~ John F. Kennedy

If we are not truly grateful for what we have, we will never be grateful for what we receive. Having gratitude for what we have currently is a must before we ask for more. Being grateful for what we have will cause us to be grateful when we eventually end up succeeding. When we are genuinely thankful for what we have, the universe will fundamentally gift us with more. If we are not, we can't expect anything to come in our favor. When we develop a stingy attitude with what we have, we are automatically saying that we are better than somebody else in some respect because of our material goods, and that does not signify gratitude in any way, shape, or form. No one is better than anybody else just because of material goods; it actually makes our character worse in the long run. That is when people ultimately look down upon you, instead of looking up to you and admiring you for who you are and what you are a success in. When your successes gift you with plentiful abundance, stay humble and be thankful for what you have.

Staying humble and grateful for what you have will only open up more opportunities for success.

Always remember and give gratitude to those that helped you along the way too. No one genuinely succeeds on their own; there are always people that have helped you get to where you are today. Gratitude doesn't merely lie in our words but in our actions as well. Show appreciation for the people that helped you get to where you are today, because without them, you wouldn't be where you are currently. I genuinely owe my success to my family. If it wasn't for their support financially, especially for the resources to be able to write this book and do other things, I definitely wouldn't be where I am today. I am also grateful for my past teachers and professors. If it weren't for them, I wouldn't have the knowledge that I have today, or be able to pay it forward in the form of a book. I thank my friends and coworkers as well, for their unwavering support in the form of love and unlimited amounts of advice when I needed it the most. Always pay your gratitude forward, whether it is in the form of just simple words or the act of carrying it out with a gesture of kindness—something small can go a long way. Be grateful for those who have made an impact on you and helped you climb the ladder of success, for it is those people in the world that you owe the most to. When you become successful, always give back, and show them that they were important figures in your life and your endeavors. Everyone that you meet in life is important and has a purpose, and this is a huge way of paying it forward and showing them that they are important too.

We also need to be grateful for life in general. As I have stated in previous chapters, the chance of us even having a life is slimmer than winning the Powerball, which means that even having a life is extremely rare and should not be taken for granted. I value my life every day, and it is something that I value the most in this world, because some people don't even get the chance to have one. For some people, if they do, they may not even be given much of a chance to live it, due to some debilitating disease. Once we realize that life is valuable, and we become grateful for it, this is the moment where we actually realize what limited time we have to become successful. Every waking moment we have, we will never get back, and the minute that we realize that every second is precious, is the moment we can actually start living our lives and do something about it. This is when a lot of people start making every experience the best that they ever had, because they start realizing the great importance of their time. This is when we best learn how to utilize our time and stop focusing on things that won't matter five years from now. Once we can start glorifying gratitude, just as we have to start amplifying kindness, we can start showing the world how precious life is, and how important everyone else is around them.

It is easy to get caught up in the hustle and bustle of life, and in our everyday endeavors, such as work, family, and other aspects of our lives that we are a part of on a daily basis. Sometimes we have to take a step back and realize all of the great things in our lives, and genuinely appreciate what we have. Appreciate what you have while you have it, because there are some things that don't last in life. Wealth can come and go, based on the choices you make in life. So, make sure you appreciate everything you have while you currently possess it. Speaking of wealth, wealthy people are generally looked down upon by those who are not wealthy, because of their material articles. The media generally portrays wealthy people as bad individuals who don't contribute anything to society. Statistics actually show that wealthy people are overall the most giving people on the planet. Most wealthy people surprisingly become wealthy so that they can donate to larger causes, such as pediatric cancer and many other life-threatening diseases, and so that they can help fund more research towards the diseases. Giving back should primarily become the goal when you eventually do become successful. Giving back creates a positive feedback loop that makes all the people that are involved, happy in some respect. Let's say that you just recently donated a few thousand dollars to St. Jude's Children's Research Hospital, once you became financially successful. Wouldn't you be happy that you just donated to such a great cause? In turn, wouldn't all of the children and doctors of St. Jude's be extremely grateful for your major contribution to their institution? This essentially creates a positive feedback loop that makes everyone happy. Let's face it; if you become financially wealthy within your journey to success, and you're not sharing with others or giving back for your success, you are just keeping everything to yourself. Learn to share the wealth! Otherwise, you will be just labeled as plain greedy. It is okay to be a little greedy and want more from a financial standpoint, as long as you give back to help others in return. That's what matters the most. Always remember that being successful doesn't always necessarily mean having material goods and money. Sometimes it means just being happy with what you love to do, and with what you currently have. Just being happy in general is the ultimate form of success. It is okay to have money and wealth, as long as you use it for good in the process.

Gratitude can positively impact your mental and emotional state of well-being, as well as the ability to achieve whatever it is that you want in your life. Having gratitude can change your perspective on life as well. Being open to allow gratitude into our lives can cause us to have good morals and do good things, even when it isn't required of us to do them. It makes us better people throughout our journey in the long haul. According to a study done by UCLA and the University of Miami, those who wrote down what they were grateful for, on a weekly basis, were more cheerful and optimistic about the upcoming week and what their days had in store for them, than those who didn't keep a weekly log. Research also showed that they missed fewer days at work and had significantly less doctor's visits than those who didn't keep a log about what they were grateful for every day. This is an example of how being grateful can also make us more successful and cause us to be more optimistic and happier than people who aren't. Being grateful has been linked to higher self-esteem, which also links to a higher job performance and work ethic. Moral of the story, if you want to be successful, be grateful for what you have first!

Have you ever heard the term, "What you focus on expands?" That's because it is true. Have you ever gotten out of bed in the morning and tripped on something that was on your floor? I bet the words you used after that were not so kind but ended in, "Only my luck," or "This only happens to me." Then, as the day went on, something else bad happened to you, and you used the same sentence again. It was because you were putting negative energy into what you focused on during the day. You were essentially putting a negative attitude into what you did, and you kept getting a negative outcome in return. If you want to stop this method of madness, start being more appreciative of the things that are going well within your day. This way, you open yourself up to a whole new realm of possibilities, and establish a variety of ways to tackle your day from a more positive perspective.

The best way to enforce gratefulness into your life is to say thank you, every step of the way. Whether it be receiving a paycheck from work, getting to your destination safely after driving, or saving yourself from a potential fall, gratefulness must start with being grateful for the little things in your life, before you can truly be grateful for the bigger things. Continuing to remain grateful for the smaller things in life can create a gateway for bigger and better circumstances to flow into your life. Many people take these small instances for granted and don't realize the great importance of these factors. A coworker that I used to work with always used to say, "Thank you, Jesus," after everything she did. She still does this currently, in everything she does. Whether it be making sure her kids are home safe, or even to the extent of dropping something on the floor at work, she would always say, "Thank you, Jesus." She remains thankful for all of the little things in her life, and this causes great things to flow into her life in return. Even if you are not religious, just saying thank you, in general, can go a long way and cause better things to flow into your life. I have learned a lot from my coworker, and I am eternally thankful to have her in my life. I have learned numerous things from her, and she has never steered me wrong. Learning to be thankful for the little things in life was one of them. She has always pushed me to be a better person, and would always remind me that I can do anything that I set my mind to. Today, I am proud to call her my best friend, and she is like a second mother to me; and I can never forget all of the good times we've had, and all of the things she has taught me.

Many people today take these small instances for granted and never realize how ultimately thankful they should be for them. Some people just go through life entirely ungrateful for everything they have, and they wonder why the universe never gifts them with anything else. They continue to go through life with a negative attitude, and they wonder why they are getting negative results. They don't appreciate what they have, and they complain when they don't have more, which creates a vicious cycle of negativity. Once you become appreciative of what you have, then you open yourself up to a wide range of opportunities to be gifted with greater things. When I was a teenager, like most other teenagers these days, I was ungrateful for a lot of the material things I had. When I was in high school, I would see some kids walking around with the latest iPhones, and driving around in some of the nicest cars, and I was jealous. My parents, at the time, didn't have the money to provide me with the latest technology or the best looking car, because the family business at the time was in a very rough spot. While other kids had the latest iPhones and were riding around in Cadillacs or brand new Jeeps, I was driving around in a 2003, bright cherry red Honda Civic, with over 211,000 miles. The phone I was carrying around was a touch screen that flipped open to an alternate screen with a physical keyboard on the other side. Compared to everyone else, I felt embarrassed. But that was my first mistake. Comparing yourself to other people shouldn't even exist. Everyone is on a different path than you, and you don't want the same things that they want. Comparing yourself to others is just a formula that sets you up for failure. As time went on and I grew older, naturally, like most people, I grew wiser as well. When I got into college, I realized that not everybody had the same cool things as everyone else did. Some people drove away in better cars, and some people had cars that looked wrecked; they were dented so badly that you didn't know if it was even legal to drive around in them. Some people had the latest iPhone, and some people didn't even have a cell phone or a car. This is when I started appreciating the small things that I had in my life. When I was in high school and complaining about the car that I did have, I started realizing that I might not have had a car at all, or a phone for that matter. The car had gotten me where I needed to go, and the phone did for me what it needed to do. It did the bare minimum, which was to make phone calls and send out texts. As time went on through college, I got my own job and started building my own credit. Once that Honda finally hit its breaking point, I had to buy another car. Today, I am driving around in a fairly new Mercedes C300, and I have a basic iPhone 6s. They are both fairly new, but they do what I need them to do. As you get older, you have the freedom to make your own choices. I chose to make my circumstances better than they were in high school, when I didn't have the means to buy my own things. This is why I am eternally grateful for what my parents had to offer. They did their best to make sure I had something with which to get me back and forth to school, and something with which to keep in touch with my family and friends on the daily. The truth is, they didn't have the means to get me the things that the other kids had, because they were too busy paying my tuition so that I could actually go to school and get a great education. As you get older, you realize the tidbits that make the picture a whole. You finally put together the missing piece of the puzzle that you were blindsided by as a teenager. Your brain fully stops developing at age 25, so at age 16, you may think you have it all together, but in all reality, it's a completely different ball game. This is why I remain truly thankful for my parents and their sacrifices, because without them, I wouldn't be where I am today.

Just as it is time to amplify kindness, it is time to glorify gratitude as well. We live in a generation where kindness and gratitude seem to be ignored and disregarded in today's society. The more we glorify gratitude, the more we can create a ripple effect for future generations and societies to come. We need to show the world that a simple act of gratitude can go a long way. We need to enlighten children on how to be thankful for what they have, and for what they continue to receive. In a world full of ungratefulness, we have to restore recognition. Once we can suppress ungratefulness, we can give gratefulness a chance to grow within our communities. We can bring a shimmer of light and hope back for the future when we continue to glorify gratitude in its fullest form. It's time to bring back a sense of importance to people who may feel as if they are insignificant or inferior, or as if they are standing alone against the world. We need to give back to our communities that have been abandoned of all love and solicitude, and revitalize them with optimism and prosperity, welcoming them back with open arms and compassion. There's a beacon of light that lies ahead and awaits for our society to become a whole again. Hope remains steadfast and constant in a world where it may seem as if there is none at all. Gratitude lies underneath all of the rubble that is buried deep within our souls.

But it is with that rubble that we reconstruct our neighborhoods and reclaim our gratitude, by bringing it back into society. Something that we all thought was lost, was just merely hiding underneath a sea of personalities. It's time to lift the anchor and have it rise to the surface, so that it can pour into our communities and instill within our hearts. Gratitude lies within our hearts. Gratitude lies within you. Shout it out and make it louder for everyone to hear; you become more successful yourself by showing it.

Chapter 10

Welcome to the Winners Circle

"Winning isn't everything, but wanting it is."
~ Arnold Palmer

Congratulations! If you have made it this far, you have got what it takes to have a million dollar mindset! We have discussed numerous ways to overcome different barriers such as fear, anger, and sadness, the way multi-millionaires do each and every day. On the daily, many successful people stand their ground and combat fear every day, but they learn to break their fears and old habits by allowing their mindset to override the emotion itself. The same thing can be said for anger and sadness, and how we learn to channel our emotions to use them to our advantage. You also learned how to develop a winning attitude and how to maintain it, despite all of the odds that are against you, such as failure. Failure is only a setback, and the only way to really ever fail in life is to stop trying. The more we keep a winning attitude when all of the odds are against us, the more we set ourselves up to become a successful person. Loving what you do, above all else, is the key to success. Do what you love, and the money will follow. Passion is priceless, and so are you. If you are priceless, what you love to do should be as well. We have to stop putting price tags on what we call our jobs, and start doing what makes us happy, because pure happiness can't be bought. True success lies in happiness and doing what you love to do every day, without failure. Marc Anthony quoted, *"If you do what you love, you'll never have to work a day in your life."* This is something that I honestly couldn't agree more on. The more you choose to make what you love a career, is it really considered work?

You deserve to be successful no matter what people may tell you. You get one shot at this thing called life; live it out to your fullest potential, and unleash the greatness that lies within you. In order to become a success, you must use your energy in a way to create and build momentum. The energy you create affects you and the people around you as well, so remember to keep it as positive as you can. The momentum that you build with your energy can mean the breaking point between winning and losing. If you lose your momentum, you slowly lose sight of your goals. If you keep up your momentum and increase it gradually every day, you are setting yourself up to be extremely successful in your career or business. But it all isn't complete without discipline. Discipline holds everything together by keeping you focused and committed to your goals. When you condition your mind to be disciplined, you are creating winning habits that set yourself up for further success. Kindness and gratitude ties the knot that binds everything else together, and ultimately seals the deal when it comes to having a million-dollar mindset. The more kindness we spread, the more we can show the world that it isn't a vulnerability but is something that makes us all stronger in the end. Gratitude works in the same respect. We never truly thank people enough for what they have done to help us, or genuinely appreciate their kind gestures. It's time that we change that and bring it back to a lost culture that needs to be touched by love and compassion, instead of hate and anger. We need to start showing people how valuable they truly are, instead of degrading them and tearing them down. We have to be thankful for the life that we have today, because you aren't guaranteed to have tomorrow.

Your mind is the most powerful weapon that you possess, but it can either make you extremely successful or make you immensely unsuccessful, based on how you choose to utilize it. If you use its riches in the right way, you will ultimately become successful in whatever it is that you love to do. You can also use it in the opposite respect, which is mainly not using its great resources at all, and let it tear you down to nothing. I can give you all the information there is on how to use your mindset to become successful, but if you don't implement the strategies, then you are only setting yourself up for failure. You have to be the one to make the decision on whether you want to succeed in what you do, or whether you just want to remain stagnant, like most people that are out there and don't realize that they have these advantages. If you want to be invested in the winner's circle, then implement these strategies! If you don't, implement them anyway, and I guarantee that you will love the results! The line that separates the winners from the losers is called execution. It lies between what you do and what you do not do. Taking execution and action towards your goals will fundamentally lead to success. You can get motivated all that you want, but if you do not take the action, you can slowly watch your dreams fade off into the distance. Yes, everything starts with motivation and a positive mindset, but the only thing between that and your destination is execution. If you do not execute, you will not win. It's as simple as that.

You were meant for more than just average. The chances of you having been born were slimmer than winning the Powerball, and yet 99% of people don't know what they are actually worth, enough to say that something needs to change! You deserve better than where you are currently, and you have all of the riches you will ever need to become successful; you just have to take advantage of them. There is a reason why most people don't go through with their dreams. It's not actually because they are scared of losing; it's because they are scared of winning. They are fundamentally scared of handling success and all of the responsibilities that comes with it. Fear is a mindset, just like everything else that we experience emotionally. The more you let fear take control of you, the more you can kiss your dreams goodbye, because fear is the number one emotion that holds people back from what they are truly capable of becoming. Once you eradicate fear, you automatically eliminate 85% of the bull that's holding you back. Losers quit when they fail, and winners fail until they succeed. Keep persisting on, even if you feel as though you are tired. That is the territory in which winners are made. True warriors never give up, and real champions never back down. When you recognize that you have nothing to lose, you just keep on gaining.

You have the ultimate power to create joy, happiness, and abundance in your life. But nothing comes easy. Throughout your journey, you will be told "no," get rejected, and have people that really mattered to you at one point, turn on you. You will have to make sacrifices you won't like to make, let people go that you don't want to let go, and love and hurt all at the same time so that you have the ability to grow. It's through the pain that we find out who we truly are. It's through the suffering that we find the best version of ourselves and what we are good at. We do our best to stay alive and fight for the common good. At the end of the day, we do all of this to improve who we are as a person, and to understand ourselves a little bit better than we did yesterday. Sometimes in losing who we are, we find someone new. At times, we are meant to lose who we are in order to find a greater potential that lies underneath the rubble of our falls. There is a light in the darkness, waiting to be found; a silence in the night as we search for a sound.

As humans, we keep persisting, keep fighting, and keep looking to a better future for tomorrow. Life is the best teacher; it hands you the test before it gives you the lesson. It is in our mistakes that we learn and grow; we find parts of us that we didn't know existed. It is in falling that we fight our toughest battles, and in rising that we find our strengths. But it's how we keep persevering through life that matters the most. How we rise after we fall, characterizes us as a true winner. It's not just in what we create and what we do to become successful. It's how we handle the rejections, how we deal with the pain of letting go, and how we move through life whilst being told "no." Life is about moving forward through the pain and suffering, and recognizing that it makes us a stronger person in the end. Through all the *no's*, we find the one *yes*; through all the heartaches, we find our best, and it's through all our failures that we finally achieve success.

In being told that we can't, this is when we finally can. Our mind is something that keeps us moving forward through all of the pain and hurt that we endure throughout our lifetime. You never fully realize its strength until you do something that you'd never thought that you'd be able to do. Nothing is impossible when we put our minds to the test. It could be our best friend or our worst enemy, our friend or our foe, depending on how we choose to take advantage of it. There are many that use its riches for the best, and also many others that use it towards their downfall. There are pros and cons to almost everything in life, but it's how we see the upside of things that really changes our perspective towards a better and brighter future. Optimism conquers pessimism, and love defeats hate. Kindness trumps animosity, and gratitude destroys condemnation. In our willingness to change our perspective, we can see the world in a whole new light that we've never seen before. Be open to different perspectives and opinions of those around you as well. Be willing to learn and expand your mind, because in doing so, we only make ourselves more successful. There's nothing that we can't learn when we open our minds to new ideas and different strategies.

Always be yourself throughout your journey. There is nothing else worse than faking to be somebody that you aren't. That "fake it until you make it" motto, is garbage advice. True winners *face* it until they make it. Face the pain, face the blows, and face getting knocked on your ass once in a while. If you go through life faking your emotions, you are not expressing the truth, and you are just lying to yourself and everyone else around you in the long run. You have to face things and let the poison out when you need to. It is in being yourself that true success will find you. Admire who you are, and take pride in the fact that you want to use the riches of your mind to become successful. You should be proud of yourself that you chose to be one of the very few who chose to go through with your success. Not many make it, but I have faith in you that you will. All it takes is having a positive, powerful mindset and a dream. Half of the battle is all mental, and once you can grasp that concept, you put yourself on the right track to become who you've always wanted to become. You can finally become the best version of you and find parts of you that you didn't even know existed.

If you want to be successful, you have to be willing to take on the treacherous journey that comes with it. You will have more obstacles than you will wins, but it's also how you view those obstacles that determines how strong your mind is. You can either see obstacles as obstacles, or you can see them as opportunities to learn from your mistakes, and adopt a different strategy the next time around. We are all worthy of success; it's just that some put the effort and hard work into it while others play around and make excuses. It all comes down to how dedicated we are every single day, and how devoted we are to being successful in what we do, which is why finding your passion is so crucial to your success. When you love what you do, it makes it a million times easier to find the energy and to condition your mind to form healthy habits and strategies to achieve your goals. Greatness exists within all of us. But greatness is not just something that we have; it is something that we can give. If you want your success to shake the world, you have to be willing to share your greatness with others as well. Depending on what you do, it could mean utilizing different strategies such as YouTube, Instagram, podcasts, or even books, to get your message out to the world. Also note that the minute you stop, it is the minute that someone else is trying to take your place and become the next best thing to ever exist with their product or brand. This is why implementing these strategies is so important. It sets your mindset up for success, and when you have control of your mind and your emotions, that is half of the battle. The other half of the battle is execution and putting in the hard work to make your dreams a reality. Anything is possible when you acquire a million-dollar mindset!

But you have to get up and fight the battle every day, because if you don't, you're already losing to life. You have to find the strength, the endurance, the power, and the stamina, to fight for something you want, and never let that dream go. Conquer it. Show everyday life who's in control, and don't let it beat you down. Rise after the fall, and work hard for what you earn. Nobody has the power to take that dream away from you. You're in control of your own life, so take control of that ship and show it who's captain. You steer yourself towards your own destiny. Every one of you has a dream, so go out there and get it. Dreams don't achieve themselves, just as a car won't drive itself. You have to go out and make that happen for yourself. Always go for the gold, and never give up, never give in, and never look away. Keep looking forward, and keep moving forward to a better today, and better yet, to a superior tomorrow. Pessimists look down, optimists look up, and realists look forward. Success doesn't come without hard work or motivation. Earn it, seize it, and keep your eyes on the vision.

You are the only one that is hindering yourself from being successful, and it's because you need to find the right tools within the toolshed to do so. The riches of your mind are the tools that you need to use if you want to become successful. Some of you may not realize that your mind is the biggest and most valuable asset that you possess for free. The moment we begin to understand that it is our most valuable asset, is the moment we can actually start using it to our advantage in a way that serves us. Malcom X once quoted, *"When your mind is a weapon, you are never unarmed."* This man was brilliant beyond any doubt. The mind is our most powerful weapon that we possess, and with it, we can never go unarmed. Our knowledge is something that can never be physically taken away from us, unlike every other material object that we own. Your mind has the power to take over the world if you let it. It can bring good fortune or have the capacity to tear it down. It has the ability to demolish cities and rebuild them all over again. Your mind is the most powerful thing that you will ever own in your lifetime. Keep it locked, loaded, and ready to fire that flame of passion inside of you that is yearning to come out. All you have to do is execute and pull the trigger.

Everyone has something that they are passionate about; you just have to go out there and figure out what it is that drives your spirit. You have to ignite that flame of passion inside of you that is burning to be let out. Let it spread like a wildfire and warm the hearts of thousands of others all across the globe. You have the power to make an impact and leave a legacy like no other man has done before. Taking advantage of the gift you were born with, is the only tool you will ever need, along with passion and a vision. Stand up for what you believe in, even if it means standing alone. Never stop fighting for what you love, and show the world what you are capable of. When you show the world what you are proficient in, give it your best and nothing less. Look up to the world with optimism and hope, instead of pessimism and disbelief. We can change the world with our minds, as long as we never allow the world to change us. Always remain true to yourself, and let your dreams bring out the best in you. Strive to become the best version of yourself every day, and never stop improving upon what you do. Master the art of what you love, and soar to new heights. The past cannot be changed, but the future is yet in your power. We are limitless to what we can achieve, and boundless of all possibilities. The only limitation we acquire is the limitation we provide ourselves. Pursue to break those limitations, and rise to no extent. Explore the world, and never stop growing in knowledge. The world is too beautiful to go unseen, and the mind too massive to go unexplored. Experience like you've never lived. Love like you have never been loved. Sing as if you have never sung. And succeed as though you have never won.

Made in the USA
Middletown, DE
25 June 2020